THE ULTIMATE GUIDE TO
SNAKES & REPTILES

THE ULTIMATE GUIDE TO
SNAKES & REPTILES

DEREK HALL

LORENZ BOOKS

This edition published in 2011 by Lorenz Books,
an imprint of Anness Publishing Ltd,
Hermes House, 88–89 Blackfriars Road,
London SE1 8HA, UK; tel. 020 7401 2077;
fax 020 7633 9499

www.lorenzbooks.com;
www.annesspublishing.com

UK distributor: Book Trade Services;
tel. 0116 2759086; fax 0116 2759090;
uksales@booktradeservices.com;
exportsales@booktradeservices.com
Australian distributor: Pan Macmillan Australia;
tel. 1300 135 113; fax 1300 135 103;
customer.service@macmillan.com.au
New Zealand distributor: David Bateman Ltd;
tel. (09) 415 7664; fax (09) 415 8892

ETHICAL TRADING POLICY
Because of Anness Publishing's ongoing
ecological investment programme, you, as our
customer, can have the pleasure and reassurance
of knowing that a tree is being cultivated on
your behalf to naturally replace the materials
used to make the book you are holding.
For further information about this scheme,
go to www.annesspublishing.com/trees

PUBLISHER'S NOTE
Although the information in this book is
believed to be accurate and true at the time
of going to press, neither the authors nor the
publisher can accept any legal responsibility
or liability for any errors or omissions that
may have been made.

CONTENTS

CHAPTER ONE
WHAT IS A REPTILE?

To many, the word 'reptile' is synonymous with sinister or repellent. It evokes a malevolent, slithery creature, slimy and cold to the touch, that dwells in dark places and is deadly poisonous. Since biblical times and before, the serpent has been the very personification of the Devil, a subtle and insidious temptor and a catcher of souls. So many reptile-like dragons and monsters abound in legends and fairy tales that they have become part of the collective unconscious and the very archetypes of evil.

The truth of the matter is that they are not slimy and they have dry skins. However, they can feel cold when touched, which may give the impression of sliminess or clamminess. Although reptiles sometimes lurk in cool, dark places, many prefer warm, sunny spots – including hot deserts – and others are to be found in the sea or in fresh water. There is no escaping the fact that snakes slither and crawl, however, and even lizards have a scuttling form of locomotion. Most reptiles eat dead or living animal tissue, and it is certainly true that human beings have sometimes ended up as meals for alligators, crocodiles, Komodo dragons (a type of large lizard) and even snakes. But as we shall see later, by far the biggest threat to human life comes from being bitten when a disturbed snake tries to defend itself in the only way it can. Most reptiles avoid human beings whenever they can.

For many years, the naming and classification (placing in groups) of animals and plants remained a more or less established and fairly static science. Whenever new species were discovered, they were named and then either classified within one of the existing groups or, if unlike anything already known to science, were assigned to a new group. Recently, however, advances in DNA analysis have caused a radical rethink of the old plant and animal family trees. One of the results of this has been that some species are now not only placed in different groups by some scientists, but have also been given different names according to which system of classification is being used. DNA comparisons have also thrown up evidence to show that, sometimes, different populations of what were originally considered to be one species are, in fact, completely separate species or a population of organisms whose members breed with each other to produce fertile offspring.

Because of this new data, the classification of many living things is in a state of flux, and figures stated by some taxonomists (people who classify living things) for the total numbers of species in certain families are often at variance with those stated elsewhere. Even the number of families may vary according to which system of classification is used; some systems combine the members of two or more families into one large family if the differences between them are not considered great enough to warrant separation, with the result that figures quoted in this book may sometimes differ from those in other publications.

WHAT IS A REPTILE?

*Nile crocodile (*Crocodylus niloticus*). The crocodile loses heat as it rests with its jaws agape. This allows it to keep cool.*

Furthermore, about 60 new reptile species are still described each year, adding to the confusion.

All reptiles, including extinct ones, are placed in the class Reptilia in which the group of animals known as vertebrates, or animals with backbones, belong. Vertebrates include most of the large, complex and highly advanced animals in the world, including the fish, the amphibians (animals such as frogs, salamanders and toads), the birds and the mammals. Depending on which authorities' figures are used, there are between about 7,770 and 8,160 species of reptiles living today – only a fraction of the number that existed during their peak, the Age of Reptiles, that lasted from about 248 to 65 million years ago. (It is worth remembering that this period represents the time when reptiles were the dominant forms on Earth; in fact, they were in existence even before this time, and of course continue to exist in smaller numbers today.)

Living reptiles are grouped into four categories known as orders. The order Chelonia or Testudines contains the turtles, tortoises and terrapins. The order Squamata is divided into three groups: the lizards, the snakes, and the curious, burrowing worm-lizards or amphisbaenids. Next comes the order Rhynchocephalia which contains just two species of the tuatara, a lizard-like reptile confined to a few islands off New Zealand, and the sole survivor of an order that evolved about 220 million years ago. Finally, there is the order Crocodylia, comprising the crocodiles, alligators, caimans (caymans) and the gharial.

Reptiles are also recognized and classified into other major subdivisions, known as subclasses, according to the nature of the openings between the bones in the temporal region (the region behind the eye sockets in the skull), there being four different variants of these openings, which are known as apses. In the subclass Anapsida there is no apse present, and the skull is therefore solid in the temporal region. This is considered to be

Giant tortoise (Geochelone elephantopus vandenburghii) *on the floor of Alcedo Crater, Isabela, Galapagos, with fumarole behind.*

*American alligator (*Alligator mississippiensis*). This alligator has hauled itself out of the water and onto a grassy knoll in the Okefenokee swamp in Georgia, U.S.A. Sunbathing helps the alligator to raise its body temperature and thus remain active.*

*Bony plates embedded in the scaly skin of a Nile crocodile (*Crocodylus niloticus*).*

the most primitive condition, and it is found in the turtles and tortoises. In the subclass Synapsida there is a single opening behind the eye socket, but there are no living synapsid reptiles. The synapsids encompass the mammal-like reptiles which evolved into the mammals during the course of evolution. The skulls of reptiles belonging to the subclass Euryapsida also show one temporal opening, but it appears high on the skull. All euryapsids are also extinct, and included the marine reptiles of the Mesozoic period such as the ichthyosaurs. The final subclass, the Diapsida, includes reptiles with two skull openings. This subclass includes the majority of reptiles, both

*Ocellated lizard (*Lacerta lepida*).
Close-up of skin showing scales and
cryptic coloration.*

living and extinct. For example, it encompasses
the lizards, snakes and crocodilians, as well as
the long-gone dinosaurs and the flying reptiles
known as pterosaurs.

Living reptiles range in size from the
tiny jaragua lizard or dwarf gecko
(*Sphaerodactylus ariasae*), at no more than

0.6-in (16-mm) long, up to the reticulated
python (*Python reticulatus*) of South-East
Asia that often exceeds lengths of 30ft (9m).
Although not quite as long, the estuarine
crocodile (*Crocodylus porosus*) of Asia and
Australia can reach 23ft (7m) in length and
is the heaviest of all living reptiles. However,

the maximum dimensions of living reptiles
are insignificant compared with the sizes
attained by some of the dinosaurs, the
long-extinct relatives of today's reptiles,
the largest of which reached lengths of 160ft
(49m) or more and may have weighed
about 100 tons.

Most biologists recognize about 17 orders of reptiles, although all but the four orders mentioned above have now become extinct and are known only from fossil evidence. Nevertheless, even the reptiles still living today show an enormous variety of body forms and have a great array of different lifestyles. Reptiles have adapted well to life in most parts of the world and rank as one of the most interesting and important of all groups of animals. In some places, like deserts, reptiles are the most successful group of animals.

Reptiles arose from amphibian ancestors in prehistoric times. They represented a huge evolutionary advance over the amphibians, and for many millions of years flourished and became the most dominant and varied creatures on earth, successfully invading the sea and the air as well as the land. There were two key factors in the success of the reptiles. First, unlike their amphibian ancestors, they laid eggs with waterproof coverings, which meant that they no longer needed to return to water to lay eggs so that the life cycle could pass through an aquatic larval stage. Instead, the embryo developed inside the moist, stable environment within the shell. Second, reptiles had a waterproof, scaly skin.

Multipurpose Scales
Apart from helping to prevent water loss from the body, the scales on a reptile also have other functions. For example, the scaly skin acts as a tough, protective barrier for the

*Green turtle (*Chelonia mydas*), showing the flattened limbs adapted for swimming in the ocean.*

*Desert monitor (*Varanus griseus*), photographed in the Sahara Desert. This endangered lizard has its nostrils close to its eyes, rather than on the tip of its snout, to help it breathe more easily when burrowing in the sand.*

internal body organs against the outside world, and also gives reptiles a degree of protection from their enemies – especially when the skin also includes protective spines like the ones seen on the backs and tails of many iguanas. Sometimes the scales of the skin are reinforced with bony plates to give extra protection, the nobbly outgrowths seen on the skin of crocodiles being a good example of these.

The scales are frequently pigmented with colours that aid camouflage. For example, the skin of the eastern green mamba (*Dendroaspis viridis*) of Africa is – as the name would suggest – green. The colour helps it to remain concealed among the leaves of the trees it inhabits as it searches for lizards and birds to eat. Chameleons (a kind of lizard) can control the pigmentation in their skins so that the colour always matches that of their surroundings – a highly effective form of camouflage. Some reptiles have vivid warning colours that signal to would-be predators that they are dangerous and should be avoided. Such warning colours are clearly seen in the eastern coral snake (*Micrurus fulvius*) of North American forests, its body marked with black, red and yellow bands. Colour may also be used to attract mates when breeding: the males of some lizard species have well-developed crests on their necks, backs or tails that may also be important when seeking a potential mate. Most snakes also use their scales to get a grip on tree trunks or on the ground when they are

*A pair of smooth snakes (*Coronella austriaca*). The female is slightly larger and is a uniform silver grey colour, while the male is more of a reddish-brown.*

A male green garden lizard in normal green phase, sen in Sinharaja National Park, Sri Lanka. The crest of scales along the back helps protect the lizard and may be used as a signal to others.

WHAT IS A REPTILE?

to be replaced and allows the reptile to grow. Usually, snakes slough all their old skin off in one piece, starting at the nose; the snake rubs away the old skin with its head, then wriggles out of it. By contrast, lizards cannot remove their skins in one piece because the legs get in the way. Instead, skin flakes off in bits and pieces over the course of several days.

The skin of a reptile has few glands, unlike that of fish, amphibians and mammals. There is a pair of glands found in the throat of crocodilians, however, and they produce a musky secretion that is probably involved in sexual activity. A few species of freshwater turtles, such as the musk turtle (*Sternotherus odoratus*), have glands in their chin or in the

LEFT
Fossil replica of an agamid lizard from the Eocene period, showing skull and lower jaw.

moving along. Geckos (another kind of lizard) can climb smooth, vertical walls with ease because they possess fine bristles on their toe pads that give them a secure grip (the bristles are modified scales). Many an inexperienced traveller in tropical climes has been alarmed to find a gecko climbing up the wall or on the ceiling of their hotel room – sometimes uttering the strident 'gek-oh' call from which the lizards get their name. But perhaps the most famous adaptation of scales is seen in the highly venomous rattlesnakes, where specially modified scales at the end of the tail are shaken or rattled to produce the familiar warning sound.

From time to time a reptile sheds its skin, new skin growing from cells beneath. Shedding enables worn-out or damaged skin

LEFT
*An ichthyosaur (*Ichthyosaurus intermedius*) of the Jurassic period. Although a reptile, this fish-eating creature had many skeletal adaptations similar to today's dolphins (mammals).*

A dwarf chameleon on a finger tip, found in the leaf litter in open forest near Zomba, Malawi.

When the skeletons of a tortoise, a lizard and a snake are compared, the differences reflecting each animal's way of life are clear to see. A tortoise is easily recognized by its shell, which is composed of horn and bone, dome-shaped on the top and flattened beneath. The backbone of the tortoise is fused to the inner surface of the top of the shell, with the limb bones attached to it. The tortoise's shell is effectively a protective box into which the animal can retreat by drawing in its head and limbs if danger threatens. It is so tough that few predators can get through it, and the tortoise remains safe inside until the danger passes. The shell has disadvantages, however. It is heavy and cumbersome and requires short, stout legs to support its weight. Movement can at best be described as 'steady progress', as anyone who has seen a tortoise in motion will testify. It has also prevented chelonians from colonizing trees or burrowing underground in the way that groups like the lizards or the snakes have done; instead, many chelonians have taken to the water, where the effort of carrying a weighty shell about is considerably reduced.

The skeletal plan of lizards most closely resembles that of the first true land reptiles. The head bears sharp teeth, and the vertebral skeleton usually terminates in a long tail. The fore- and hindlimbs are relatively long compared with those of a tortoise, allowing for fairly efficient movement as a result. As we shall see later, there are other skeletal adaptations among the lizards designed to

region of their hindlimbs, while some non-venomous snakes can secrete an irritant material from glands situated under the scales of the neck. Its purpose may be defence, although it has been suggested that it may also play a role in mating. Geckos of the genus *Diplodactylus* can squirt sticky filaments from glands under the scales of the tail, possibly as a deterrent to enemies.

Inside the Reptile Body

The reptile skeleton and internal body plan has been modified considerably during the course of evolution to suit different modes of life. It also shows considerable variation among the reptiles living today for the same reason. Unlike the amphibians, most reptiles possess sharp, pointed teeth which are replaced throughout their life when they become worn or damaged. The chelonians (turtles and tortoises) did away with teeth early on in their evolution, but they have horny beaks which also continue to grow throughout the life of the animal.

*A saltwater or estuarine crocodile (*Crocodylus porosus*) at the Kakadu National Park, Australia.*

assist them in their varied ways of life. They include modifications for climbing, running and even for gliding through the air.

In terms of their skeletal structure, snakes are the most highly modified of all reptiles. The backbone is extremely long and flexible, consisting of up to 400 vertebrae in some of the longer species. The vertebrae are specially strengthened to withstand the extra pressures imposed upon them by the muscles. One of the most remarkable features of a snake is its ability to swallow huge prey without biting it into pieces first – a feat it can achieve because of the special way in which the bones of the two halves of the jaw are connected together

RIGHT
*The tail, showing detail of scales, of a Nile crocodile (*Crocodylus niloticus).

OPPOSITE
*This marine iguana (*Amblyrhynchus cristatus) *has hauled itself out onto a rock in the Galapagos Islands. Special nasal glands enable it to remove excess salt from the body, taken in during diving and eating seaweeds.*

WHAT IS A REPTILE?

(see page 278). But perhaps the most remarkable feature of all is the fact that snakes have done away with limbs altogether, relying instead on muscular body movements to get around. Inefficient though this may seem, snakes have in fact perfected the technique to an astonishing degree and can move effectively on land, under ground, in trees and even in water. Using a similar method to the one used by certain species of

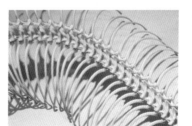

OPPOSITE
Nile crocodile (Crocodylus niloticus).

LEFT
The skeleton of a Cook Strait tuatara (Sphenodon punctatus), showing skull and large orbital socket and horny beak on the upper jaw. Tuataras are only to be seen in New Zealand.

FAR LEFT
Detail of the skin of the western rattlesnake (Crotalus viridis).

LEFT
Vertebrae of a boa constrictor.

*This parrot snake (*Leptophis depressirostris*), merges almost invisibly into the green foliage. La Selva, Costa Rica.*

A radiated tortoise (Geochelone radiata) *in Madagascar. Many land tortoises have high-domed shells to prevent predators from closing their jaws around them.*

lizard, there are even some types of snake that can hurl themselves from one tree and glide through the air to another.

The skeletons of reptiles have several bones not found in mammals. For example, the eyes of lizards, the tuatara (*Sphenodon* species) and the turtles have bony plates called scleral ossicles that help in focusing, while in the crocodilians and the tuatara, special abdominal ribs are present that help to reinforce the belly wall.

Reptiles have the same basic collection of internal organs that are found in other vertebrates, including brains and other sense organs such as eyes, a heart, lungs, kidneys, a digestive system with a stomach, pancreas, liver and intestine, and reproductive organs. However, as with other parts of the body, the

The head of a tuatara (Sphenodon punctatus)*, showing pupil tightly closed by day. Stephens Island, New Zealand.*

*Male Namibian rock lizard (*Agama planiceps*).*

*Nile monitor (*Varanus niloticus*), showing forked tongue that helps it to sample minute scent particles in the air.*

organs are often modified to suit the lifestyle of the reptile concerned. Some snakes, for example, have only one lung instead of the more usual pair.

Some reptiles have additional, special organs not found in other vertebrates. For example, snakes and a few lizards have a special sensing organ, called Jacobson's organ, situated in the roof of the mouth. When a reptile constantly flicks its tongue in and out, it is actually picking up scent particles in the air or from the ground. These are then passed back to the Jacobson's organ for analysis. By doing this, the reptile learns all it needs to know about its environment. It can locate food, track down a mate or detect an enemy. Some snakes, such as pythons and pit vipers, can detect the infrared heat given out by warm-blooded prey, and can locate them even in conditions of complete darkness.

Most lizards have good eyesight. Iguanas can perceive colour, and this is why some species have bright, colourful crests, throat pouches and other adornments that they use for communication with one another. Hearing is also well-developed in most reptiles. Lizards have ear openings which are visible on the sides of their head, and through which they hear airborne sounds. Snakes, on the other hand, use the bones in their skulls to pick up vibrations from the ground, which are then passed to the inner ear.

One of the most remarkable examples of reptilian senses is the feat of navigation shown by the green turtle (*Chelonia mydas*).

It spends its adult life grazing on seagrass meadows off the Brazilian coast, but each year migrates 1,300 miles (2100km) to breed on Ascension Island in the Atlantic Ocean. How does the turtle find its unerring way to the island, which is only 5 miles (8km) across? Scientists believe that somehow it uses magnetic fields to find its way and can detect the scent of its destination as it draws near.

A Cold-Blooded Life
Reptiles are described as cold-blooded, though this does not mean that their blood is always cold. However, reptiles cannot maintain a constant body temperature because, unlike mammals or birds, they have no fur or feathers to insulate them and retain their body heat. They also have a low metabolic rate which means it is difficult to generate their own internal body warmth in the first place. Instead, reptiles rely on the temperature of their surroundings to warm their bodies and enable them to become active. This is the reason why most reptile species are found in warm, sunny parts of the world, although some are adapted to life in cooler regions; in fact, Antarctica is the only continent where no reptiles are found at all.

In order to speed up the body-warming process, reptiles often bask in the sun. On a sunny morning, a lizard will crawl out of its hiding place, climb on top of a large rock and position itself so that it can feel the full warmth of the sun's rays. After a while its

The spiny-footed lizard (Acanthodactylus erythrurus)*, has little fringes on its feet which enable it to run on loose desert sand without sinking in.*

RIGHT
*Black girdle-tailed lizard (*Cordylus
niger) *in Cape Province, South
Africa.*

OPPOSITE
*Mojave fringe-toed lizard (*Uma
scoparia)*, photographed in southern
California.*

WHAT IS A REPTILE?

RIGHT
*Cook Strait tuatara (*Sphenodon
punctatus) *on Takapourewa,
(Stephens Island), New Zealand.*

OPPOSITE
*The boomslang (Dispholidus typus)
is a venomous tree snake from South
Africa whose bite can be fatal. It
hunts during the day for small
vertebrates, aided by its excellent
vision. A minute amount of its potent
haemotoxic venom quickly kills its
victims by causing haemorrhaging.*

body will be warm enough and it can go in search of food. However, during the hottest parts of the day it may seek shade to cool down a little – even a reptile can get too hot – but when it becomes too cool in the shade, the lizard simply gets back in the sun to warm up again. In this way, it keeps its body at an optimum temperature for activity. In very hot conditions, a reptile spends more time in the shade than in the sun; it also needs warmth to help digest its food. A snake that has eaten a large meal will die if it cannot keep its body warm, because the food will not digest properly in the intestines and will rot.

Warm-blooded animals can regulate their internal body temperatures by various methods. For example, if they are too hot, they can pant or sweat, if too cold, they can shiver to generate heat or fluff up their fur or feathers to trap a warm layer of air near the skin. They can also control the way in which heat is lost through the blood vessels. Reptiles also have some physiological methods of regulating temperature. In the early part of the day, hormones cause pigments in the skin to spread and thus darken the body which, since dark surfaces absorb heat more readily, helps to warm up the reptile more quickly.

Because they are less dependent on maintaining a high body temperature, reptiles do not need to eat large quantities of food to 'stoke the furnace'. A typical reptile can make do with 30 to 50 times less food than a

warm-blooded animal (in other words, a bird or a mammal) of the same size. Many reptile species can therefore live in places where food is scarce, such as deserts, and need to use energy only when seeking, eating or digesting food. Even then, many reptiles simply lie in wait and ambush their prey to save energy.

Among reptiles, lizards prefer the warmest temperatures. Some species are active at temperatures as high as 107° F (42° C). The lizard with the lowest temperature requirement is the tuatara (*Sphenodon* species), which lives in New Zealand. Its usual activity range is 43–61° F (6–16° C).

Reptiles that live in cooler parts of the world cannot keep their bodies sufficiently warm in winter to maintain activity. Therefore, like several other types of animals living in cold places, they hibernate. Hibernation is often thought of as a form of deep sleep, although in reality it is more complex. Hibernating animals enter a dormant state in which the body processes slow down considerably. Reptiles must find a safe place in which to hibernate before winter sets in. The site needs to be somewhere dry and preferably warm, but also somewhere that predators cannot access. Hibernating reptiles may choose holes in banks and cracks between rocks, or crawl under logs and large stones. Rattlesnakes often hibernate together in large groups, coiled around each other to help stay warm. Reptiles living in the tropics sometimes enter a state of inactivity during dry periods when food is scarce. This is called aestivation and resembles hibernation.

Venomous Reptiles

A characteristic of many snakes, and also just a few species of lizards, is the ability to produce venom or poison. The venom is designed to paralyse or kill the reptile's prey before it is swallowed, but it is also an effective weapon of self-defence. Poisonous snakes are found worldwide in all kinds of habitats including the sea, where some of the most venomous snakes of all live. The majority of venomous snakes are found in the tropics, however, with some species able to use their deadly toxin as soon as they hatch from their shells. Venomous snakes use specially modified fangs to puncture the victim's skin before the poison is injected.

The south-western U.S.A. and Mexico are home to the world's only poisonous lizards: the beaded lizard (*Heloderma horridum*) and the Gila monster (*Heloderma suspectum*). They use their poison for attack rather than for defence, their method of delivering it being less sophisticated than that of snakes. The venom is released from salivary glands in the mouth and enters the prey when the lizard bites.

Reptile Food

Most reptiles are meat-eaters. Even if one was not familiar with their lifestyle, the large, daggerlike teeth of crocodiles would hardly suggest any other form of diet. Many lizards, too, have sharp, pointed teeth, and it is true that many of them are also carnivores. Depending on the species, the food on the lizard menu includes insects, worms and other invertebrates, birds and their eggs, reptiles and mammals. However, among the agamid lizards and iguanas, for example, there are many vegetarian species. Snakes, as a group, are all carnivorous, and their diet ranges from bird and fish eggs to other reptiles and large mammals such as pigs and deer. Tortoises are generally herbivorous, using their sharp, horny jaws to tear off pieces of vegetation. Anyone whose pet tortoise has escaped into the garden and got among the shrubbery and flowers will know how effective those jaws are at dealing with vegetation! But even tortoises will eat meat on occasions. Seaturtles enjoy a wide diet, including marine creatures such as crabs, jellyfish, molluscs and fish, though plants are eaten sometimes. Freshwater turtles hunt for crustaceans, worms, molluscs and fish.

When feeding, the slow-moving, almost moribund state exhibited by many reptiles is immediately transformed. True, a tortoise will go about munching vegetation at much the same slow, measured speed as it does everything else, but a reptile like a chameleon can snare its prey at a speed too fast for the human eye to see. Even large cumbersome-looking creatures like alligators and crocodiles attack their prey with such speed and ferocity that they can lunge out of the water and grab a large animal like a

*The canebrake rattlesnake (*Crotalus horridus atricaudatus*) occurs in lowland areas and feeds primarily on grey squirrels. It typically feeds just once or twice a year.*

A living coil of speckled sun snakes.

*Komodo dragons (*Varanus komodoensis*) feeding on a goat.*

A Galapagos giant tortoise (Geochelone elephantopus vandenburgii) *feeding on grass.*

*Male southern rock agama (*Agama atra atra*), seen in South Africa.*

RIGHT and OPPOSITE
A green turtle (Chelonia mydas)
laying eggs on a sandy beach at
night. Turtles lay lots of eggs, due to
high mortality rates, and round eggs
are the best shape for getting a
maximum amount into a hole.

young buffalo from the bank before it has time to escape.

Most reptiles rely on their size and powerful jaws to overcome smaller prey, which is either swallowed whole or chewed a little before being swallowed. A few species, like the Komodo dragon (*Varanus komodoensis*), scavenge on the carcasses of dead animals, using their strong jaws and teeth to shear off pieces of the victim's flesh. The snakes have evolved some of the most unusual strategies for food capture among any group of animals. As we shall see later, the elapids and vipers, in particular, have developed highly toxic venom in order to subdue their prey before swallowing it. Snakes such as pythons and constrictors wrap their hugely muscular bodies around their prey and suffocate it before swallowing it down. Another astonishing feature of snake gastronomy is their ability to open their jaws so widely that they can engulf prey far larger than would seem possible. Once swallowed, the snake must find somewhere safe to rest while it digests its meal, which may take a week or more in the case of large prey.

Life from an Egg

Reptiles are not generally gregarious creatures, but they must seek out others of their own species when it is time to mate and reproduce. In most reptile species, there are differences in coloration, size or shape between the two sexes. Male lizards, tortoises and crocodilians tend to be bigger than the females, whereas in many turtles and snakes the females are larger. Many reptiles take part in complicated behavioural rituals prior to and during mating.

Among male iguanid and agamid lizards the males are usually brightly coloured, particularly in the mating season, and many possess ornate crests and frills that help to attract the females. The green anole (*Anolis carolinensis*), a forest-dwelling species found in America, can inflate a brightly-coloured red throat sac to help attract a mate. This also serves as an aggressive warning signal that tells other males to keep away. Sometimes a couple of male anole lizards will stage a 'stand-off', with each one inflating his throat sac at the other for long periods at a time. Males of other species of lizards perform similar threat displays, but many monitor lizards go one better, engaging in wrestling matches, grasping each other with their forelimbs while rearing up on their hindlegs, their tails acting as supports. The wrestling match usually ends with the weaker animal retiring to find an easier opponent. Other male lizards bob their heads up and down to attract a mate or secrete a substance that is thought to be attractive to the opposite sex.

Snakes go in for less overt methods of advertising for a partner but, like lizards, a few also secrete attractants to lure the opposite sex. However, once snakes have met up for the purposes of mating, there is often a complicated and heavily ritualized courtship display. Males may insinuate themselves

against females, the male rubbing the female's chin with his body. Sometimes, the male and females entwine their bodies, or they may rear up together. Vine snakes are long, thin snakes found in Central and northern South America. They often mate in seething groups, when the males attempt to copulate with as many females as they possibly can.

As part of their courtship, male tortoises may barge into female tortoises, or roar at them and bite their limbs. Male turtles behave in a slightly more romantic manner: they often swim in front of females and stroke them around the head in an attempt to woo them. Crocodilians also perform stroking and rubbing manoeuvres as part of their courtship display, although prior to the actual mating there is often plenty of aggressive thrashing around in the water by them both.

Fertilization takes place internally in all reptiles. In most reptiles, sperm is introduced directly into the female's cloaca by the male. In turtles, tortoises and crocodilians the males have a single penis, but in snakes and lizards the males have paired sex organs, known as hemipenes, although only one is used at a time when mating.

Temperature, daylight and other environmental factors play a large part in the breeding patterns of reptiles. Reptiles that live in cool climates usually only breed once or perhaps twice a year. Species such as the adder or common viper (*Vipera berus*), a venomous snake of northern Europe, may not even breed every year. On the other hand,

reptiles in warm, tropical climes where food is plentiful most of the time, often breed at intervals throughout the year.

Although most reptiles breed by sexual reproduction – a process involving both males and females – some species reproduce by what is known as virgin birth (parthenogenesis). In this process, populations consisting only of females seem to be able to give birth to offspring without being fertilized by sperm from a male. Among the reptiles that can reproduce this way are certain species of whiptail lizards found in North America and rock lizards living in the Caucasus of south-western Russia. Parthenogenesis is found in several different groups of animals, including several types of insects such as aphids and bees, but it is fairly rare among vertebrates and not encountered at all in birds and mammals.

A feature of reptiles, and indeed possibly the most important factor in their success as a group, is that they lay eggs. Protected safely inside the egg, provided with an inbuilt food supply and cushioned by a sac of watery fluid called the amnion, the young develop until they are ready to hatch out. The tough outer coating of the egg not only provides a high degree of protection for the developing baby reptile but, being waterproof, also prevents the contents from drying out. To enable the young reptile to hatch out, it possesses a small, sharp egg tooth, similar to that used by hatching birds, at the front of the snout, which allows the baby to cut open the eggshell. A few days

The green turtle (Chelonia mydas) *–*
so-called because its fat is green.

OPPOSITE

OPPOSITE
Sexual dimorphism in adders
(Vipera berus). *The larger female
has a brown body, while those of the
two males are predominantly white.*

LEFT
A common or viviparous lizard
(Lacerta vivipara) *shedding the
remainder of its thin-walled egg sac
after birth.*

*A male giant tortoise (*Geochelone elephantopus vandenburgii*) approaching a female in the Galapagos Islands.*

after the baby comes out of the egg, the egg tooth falls off.

However, it would be unusual to expect this large group of animals to conform to the same system when it comes to giving birth. Not only do reptile eggs vary enormously in shape, size and texture according to species, there is also great variation in the way the eggs are laid and subsequently tended. In addition, a great many snake and lizard species have done away with egg-laying altogether. Instead, they give birth to fully-developed young, in a way similar to almost all mammals. Furthermore, unlike most bird and mammal young – that can often look quite different from their parents (especially in terms of coloration) – newly-hatched reptiles look like perfectly formed, miniature versions of the adults.

Tortoises and a few turtles lay hard-shelled eggs, while those of aquatic turtles are soft, although they come onto land to lay them. The female digs a hole or scrapes a depression in the ground before laying the eggs, then covers them as protection against predators and to help keep them warm enough to incubate. The temperature at which the eggs incubate often determines the sex of the developing baby reptile. Among turtles, for example, warm eggs (above 87° F/30.5° C) produce females, while eggs that are cooler (below 82° F/28° C) are born as males.

Lizards mostly lay eggs with leathery shells which, once laid, are usually abandoned to their fate. However, some species of skinks show a degree of parental concern and use their bodies to brood the eggs they have laid. Some of the most elaborate egg-protection strategies are those exhibited by crocodilians. The female Nile crocodile (*Crocodylus niloticus*) carefully tends the eggs she has just laid, even helping to dig the young hatchlings out from the protective mound of soil in which the eggs were laid. Then, she delicately gathers each one up in her mouth and carries it to the safety of the river. American alligators (*Alligator mississippiensis*) build a mound of leaves and other vegetation in which to bury the 50 or so eggs that the female lays. The heat from the vegetation helps to incubate the eggs, as well as providing somewhere to hide them from the other prying predators that stalk the wetlands.

Among snakes that lay eggs, many simply deposit them in soil or vegetation and then abandon them in the expectation that some will survive to hatch out. But some species, such as cobras and pythons, again show a degree of parental concern, coiling themselves around the eggs to protect them and help keep them warm. Instead of laying eggs, some snakes (such as many sea snakes and some vipers and boas) and some lizards (such as some geckos) have developed live-bearing as a way of giving birth; consequently, the eggshell is reduced or has been done away with altogether. In some species, the mother retains just a thin, membranous eggshell in her body and the young are released when developed. This system is known as ovoviviparity. In other live-bearing reptiles, a kind of placenta forms inside the mother's body to enable an exchange of waste products and nutrients to take place between the mother and the developing embryo, as happens in mammals. This more 'developed' form of live-bearing is called viviparity. It is seen in most of the sea snakes as well as in reptiles that live in latitudes where temperatures are generally too low for normal egg-laying and incubation to be successful.

STAYING ALIVE

A dog out for a walk with its owner encounters a European grass snake (*Natrix natrix*) basking in the early morning sun by the side of a path. At first, the snake rears up and hisses at the dog, but instead of withdrawing the dog begins to snap at the snake. Suddenly, the snake throws itself onto its back and lies motionless with its tongue hanging out, to all intents and purposes appearing to be dead. After a few cautious sniffs, the dog loses interest and moves off. Shortly afterwards, the snake rights itself and moves quickly into the safety of the undergrowth, demonstrating that the ability to play dead is just one of the many survival techniques employed by reptiles.

Like almost all other animals, reptiles have their enemies, and much of the reptilian struggle for life is concerned with avoiding being attacked or eaten by other creatures.

*A forest or canopy lizard (*Polychrus gutturosus*) seen in Costa Rica.*

WHAT IS A REPTILE?

Even a large crocodile – a fierce predator in its own right with few natural enemies – can fall prey to other creatures, one of which is the African python (*Python sebae*), a huge constricting snake that pursues crocodiles into the water to overcome and eventually swallow them. In the natural world, the enemies of reptiles include birds, mammals, other reptiles, certain amphibians and fish. Most reptiles have at least one inbuilt defence system: they have scaly bodies that offer a degree of protection from some assailants. In the case of crocodilians, the skin provides an especially tough outer coating, and in many tortoises and turtles the shell can prove to be an almost impregnable fortress against many foes. However, beneath that scaly reptilian skin or shell is a succulent meal just waiting to be eaten by a vigilant, hungry predator.

For many reptiles, the simplest way of not being eaten is to avoid being spotted in the first place. For this reason, many reptiles are cryptically camouflaged to help them blend in with their surroundings. This is why many tree lizards, for example, are coloured green to blend in with the foliage. The skin pattern of the Gaboon viper (*Bitis gabonica*), a venomous snake from tropical Africa, is designed to match the fallen leaves and plant debris on the floor of its forest habitat. Such coloration has other advantages, of course, for this near invisibility also helps the reptile to approach its prey without being detected. Among reptiles, chameleons are the supreme masters of disguise, changing their skin

colour at will to merge with each new background on which they find themselves. Sometimes, more than simple colours are used to fool enemies. The grass-green vine snake (*Dryophis prasinus*) of Asia and India is not only coloured green to match the foliage, it also has an extremely long body – no thicker than a pencil – that resembles the vines and creepers that festoon the trees on which it lives. This makes it even harder to spot – particularly since the snake has the habit of hanging down motionless from a branch.

Often, however, defence is simply a matter of hiding away for as much of the time as possible. Many snakes and lizards are nocturnal, by day living under rocks or fallen logs, and only venturing out under cover of darkness to search for food.

Other reptiles that do not hide away or camouflage themselves may rely on the speed with which they can escape from danger. The strand racerunner (*Cnemidophorus lemniscatus*) is a 12-in (30-cm) long lizard found in flood plains and open forests in parts of Central America. It is one of the fastest of all lizards, capable of a recorded speed of up to 17mph (27km/h), sometimes running on its hindlegs. Basilisk lizards are a larger species that live in South African forests which can also cover the ground at great speed – running on their two back legs only – and can even run over the surface of water to effect an escape. For this reason, they are sometimes known as Jesus Christ lizards.

As well as the birds, all the other groups of vertebrates include members that have evolved the ability to fly through the air. However, only the birds, and among the mammals the bats, have developed flapping flight. The species of fish, amphibians and reptiles that fly do so only by gliding. However, this in itself is no mean feat, and confers upon animals possessing this ability an effective way of travelling significant distances quickly and very efficiently in terms of energy expenditure. In most instances, however, gliding flight is used as a means of rapidly escaping an enemy. Among the lizards, the 20 or so species known as flying dragons inhabit the forests of South-East Asia and southern India. When taking flight, these 10-in (20-cm) long reptiles launch themselves from a branch and, using flaps of skin supported by specially elongated ribs, glide to safety. The remarkable flying snakes glide through the air by launching themselves from a branch before flattening their bodies to give themselves a lift.

Throughout the animal kingdom, colour and pattern are used in various forms of communication, one of the most effective being the use of warning colours. These tell other animals that the wearer is dangerous – usually by virtue of the fact that it is poisonous or unpleasant to eat or possesses a venomous bite or sting. Warning colours are designed to be there for all to see, so animals are brightly patterned or marked – usually with contrasting colours that are

A green turtle hatchling emerging from its nest site on a sandy beach.

predominantly red, blue, yellow, black and white. In snakes, the contrasting colours often take the form of alternating bands of colour around the body. Thus, as we have seen, the highly toxic eastern coral snake (*Micrurus*

fulvius) of the U.S.A. is brightly marked with black, yellow and red bands. The eastern brown snake (*Pseudonaja textilis*) of Australia and New Guinea is less vividly marked, but its striking orange-brown and purple hoops

still advertise its venomous nature.

As already mentioned, the Gila monster (*Heloderma suspectum*), a large, stout-bodied lizard of the arid regions of southern U.S.A. and Mexico, is one of only two venomous

A black-tipped reef fish feeding on a baby turtle on the Great Barrier Reef, Australia.

*A grass snake (*Natrix natrix*) feigns death by hanging its head down with its mouth agape and tongue limp.*

This chameleon is well camouflaged against its background of leaves as it moves over the ground.

*A Gaboon viper (*Bitis gabonica*) in South Africa, showing disruptive coloration. Its body pattern mimics the fallen leaves, enabling it to become almost invisible.*

lizards, its body covered in an intricate, reticulated pattern of contrasting yellow and brown markings. The venom is produced in glands in the lower jaw and enters the victim when the lizard bites. Like the defensive bites from many of the venomous snakes, a bite from the venomous Gila monster is a formidable method of deterring a would-be predator.

When confronted by a potential threat, many reptiles decide to 'tough it out' instead of running away. When threatened, cobras rear up, expanding the flaps of skin around their necks or 'hoods' to make themselves appear larger. As they do so, a huge eye pattern on the back of the hood adds to the illusion. Making oneself appear larger to enemies is dramatically demonstrated by the frilled lizard (*Chlamydosaurus kingii*) of Australia and New Guinea. When alarmed, this slender, long-tailed lizard fans out an enormous, colourful ruff of skin, making the animal appear at least four times wider than it really is. The threat display is accompanied by a huge gaping mouth display, with bobbing head and much foot-stamping.

One of the most remarkable methods of self-preservation is demonstrated in certain species of lizards. In the event of a predator grabbing one of these lizards by its tail, the lizard can immediately shed it and make its escape – a process known as autotomy. This may appear to be a drastic method of escape, but to lose a tail is better than been eaten. Indeed, many lizards even wave their tails

alluringly prior to being attacked to attract the predator to this particular part of the body. The bones of the tail vertebrae have special 'fault lines' where the break can occur, the muscles and blood vessels in this region being specially modified to facilitate the process. Once detached, the tail continues to waggle about seductively for a few minutes more to encourage the attacker to persevere.

In time, however, the lizard regenerates a new tail, though it is never quite the same as the original and the bones no longer have

fracture planes, so if it breaks again it must be even higher up. Losing a tail, therefore, is not something to be taken lightly. A great deal of valuable energy is expended in growing a new one; in many lizards, moreover, valuable fat is stored in the tail to tide them over the winter or times of drought. The fat stored in a female lizard's tail also helps in egg-yolk production, and individuals that lack tails tend to produce weaker offspring that have fewer chances of survival.

*The Gaboon viper (*Bitis gabonica*) is a highly venomous and well-camouflaged snake of African rainforests.*

RIGHT
*A Cook Strait tuatara (*Sphenodon
punctatus*) emerging from a burrow
it shares with fairy prions on
Stephens Island, New Zealand.*

OPPOSITE LEFT
*A frilled lizard (*Chlamydosaurus
kingii*) photographed on the
Kimberley plateau in Western
Australia*

OPPOSITE RIGHT
*This Indian cobra (*Naja naja*) is
highly venomous. When threatened,
it will assume this characteristic
pose in which it elongates its long
flexible neck ribs and loose skin to
form the distinctive hood. It will
defend itself by forcing venom
through its fangs and, by exerting
muscular pressure on its venom
glands, will cause jets of venom to
be ejected. The 'eye' pattern on the
back of the hood is intended to fool
predators into thinking that it has a
huge head.*

*This slow-worm (*Anguis fragilis*), a legless lizard, has just shed its tail as a means of defence, an ability known as caudal autonomy.*

ENDANGERED SPECIES

In each of the following chapters devoted to the main groups of reptiles, there is an indication of how many species in each family, if any, are at risk due to factors such as destruction of habitat and general exploitation. The data is based on the IUCN (International Union for the Conservation of Nature) categories. The IUCN is the body charged with the responsibility for assigning animals and plants to internationally agreed categories of rarity and adopts the following categories:

Extinct (EX): when there is no reasonable doubt that the last individual of a species has died.

Extinct in the Wild (EW): when a species is known only to survive in captivity or as a naturalized population well outside its past range.

Critically Endangered (CR): when a species is facing an extremely high risk of extinction in the wild in the immediate future.

Endangered (EN): when a species faces a very high risk of extinction in the wild in the near future.

Vulnerable (VU): when a species faces a high risk of extinction in the wild in the medium-term future.

Lower Risk (LR): when a species has been evaluated and does not satisfy the criteria for CR, EN or VU.

Data Deficient (DD): when there is not enough information about a species to assess the risk of extinction.

Not Evaluated (NE): describes species that have not been assessed under IUCN criteria.

CHAPTER TWO

THE EVOLUTION OF REPTILES

This is a replica of an original Jurassic period fossil of pterosaur (Pterodactylus antiquus). Pterosaur is Greek for 'wing lizard' and these reptiles were able to fly using membranous wings supported by elongated fourth fingers.

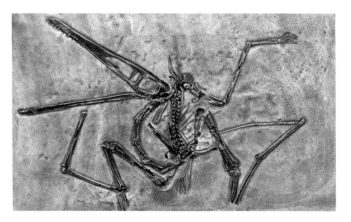

The first animals with backbones to leave the water and colonize the land were the amphibians – the group of creatures that today includes the frogs, toads, newts and salamanders. Amphibians evolved about 400 million years ago, and at first reigned supreme, flourishing in the warm, humid and swampy landscapes that covered much of the planet during the Carboniferous period. Their long supremacy was to be punctuated by the appearance of some highly dramatic examples of evolutionary experimentation. If we could be transported back to that time, we would probably have seen many species quite similar to the frogs and other amphibians we know today. However, we would have also encountered some bizarre creatures quite unlike anything alive now; for example, huge amphibians like *Mastodonsaurus*, a giant frog over 10-ft (3-m) long with a tail and jaws armed with sharp teeth. Or *Diplocaulus*, that lived in what is now Texas, an amphibian with huge, horny outgrowths on either side of its head, possibly to prevent predators from swallowing it.

About 300 million years ago, while the amphibians were still the dominant vertebrate animals on land, the first reptiles made an appearance. The direct ancestor of the reptiles is the subject of speculation, but they represented a distinct evolutionary advance over the amphibians, and there were several key factors in their success. As well as having limbs that were better adapted for walking efficiently on dry land, they possessed waterproof bodies; they also laid shelled eggs. Gone was the need to return to the water to lay vulnerable eggs, and gone was the need to undergo an aquatic larval stage before developing into an adult. Instead, the embryo formed inside the moist, stable environment enclosed within the shell. Gone, too, as an adult, was the need to stay close to water in order to avoid drying up and death. They now had a thick, tough skin made up of keratinous plates known as scales, which helped to prevent water being lost from the body by evaporation and were again crucial in that reptiles lost their reliance on damp places. Moreover, they could now colonize all kinds of new, drier land habitats that were beginning to form on earth.

However, the advanced reptilian body design still had its drawbacks. The heavy skin-covering meant that reptiles could be cumbersome on land – the shelled tortoises and turtles especially so. Reptiles had slow

THE EVOLUTION OF REPTILES

LEFT

This is a fossil replica of an eryopid (Sclerocephalus haeuseri) *of the Permian period.*

BELOW

This is a fossil of the long-tailed pterosaur, Scaphognathus crassirostris, *with head crest. It is from the Jurassic period and was found in the Solnhofen limestone region of southern Germany. Its prey was firmly held by the fish-hook teeth within the large beak.*

metabolisms and no way of retaining their body heat, which made them reliant on the heat from the sun to warm their bodies and keep them active. Even modern reptiles can only become fully active once the heat of the sun has warmed their bodies, although there is considerable speculation that some prehistoric reptiles may have been warm-blooded, like mammals and birds. Otherwise, it is difficult to explain the high levels of activity which scientists believe some prehistoric reptiles achieved, a more vigorous level than we see in modern-day examples.

In time, the reptiles' new improved body plan was to enable them to flourish and to become the most diverse, successful and long-lived group of animals ever to roam the earth. From their early beginnings, the reptiles steadily expanded in both numbers and species. Just like the amphibians before them, the reptiles produced a wealth of forms resembling some of the species we see today, but they also produced a much greater array of extraordinary and stunning evolutionary divergences. Among these were the flying pterosaurs, aquatic predators such as the ichthyosaurs and the plesiosaurs, and the most spectacular prehistoric reptiles of all, the dinosaurs. These groups may not have survived the course of evolution, but they included among them creatures of such size, mystery and power that they still fire the imagination and fill us with awe today. Furthermore, at some point during the process of evolution, the reptilian family tree gave rise to the two other, and most advanced, groups of vertebrates, the birds and the mammals. In all, the great Age of Reptiles lasted from about 280 to about 65 million years ago – a vast timescale compared with the 3 or 4 million years that human beings have been on Earth. During that time, reptiles expanded and diversified to fill all the ecological niches similar to the ones occupied by the most successful vertebrates living today, namely the birds and the mammals.

*This a replica skull of a pelycosaur (*Dimetrodon limbatus*) from the early Permian period. This mammal-like predatory reptile had a large fin or sail on its back. Note the single apse, or opening, behind the eye socket – a feature of a synapsid reptile.*

EARLY REPTILES

One of the earliest of all known reptiles is *Westlothiana lizziae*. Reconstructions of this animal, whose fossil remains were found in ancient carboniferous rocks in Scotland, show it to be somewhat of a cross between an amphibian and a reptile. *Westlothiana* had a long body and tail, like that of a typical lizard, but it also had a blunt, almost frog-like head. Other early reptiles, such as *Hylonomus*, also displayed distinct reptilian features, including small but well-defined teeth and longer legs for walking. By the start of the Permian period, about 295 million years ago, other kinds of reptiles had evolved. Just like the species living today, some of them were plant-eaters and others were carnivores. One such early plant-eater was a creature called

Scutosaurus, a lumbering, tank-like reptile about the size of a hippopotamus. *Scutosaurus* was a member of a group known as pareiasaurs. It had a skin covered with knobbly, bony plates and outgrowths and blunt, grinding teeth for coping with the tough vegetation.

Of the many evolutionary excursions undertaken by the reptiles, one of the first involved a group of synapsid reptiles called the pelycosaurs, also known as sail-fin reptiles because the vertebrae of their backbones bore long, erect spines that supported a huge flap of skin resembling a sail. It is thought that the 'sail' acted as a kind of heat conductor, enabling the pelycosaurs to warm up with the help of the sun's rays. In the early morning, a pelycosaur would turn its body so that the sail was facing full on to the sun, ensuring that the maximum amount of heat could be absorbed by its body as quickly as possible. Ready and active, the pelycosaur could now begin its quest for food. Carnivorous pelycosaurs, like the 10-ft (3-m) *Dimetrodon*, were armed with stabbing and slashing teeth for killing and eating prey, whereas herbivorous species like *Edaphosaurus* had blunt, chisel-like teeth to cope with plant food.

About 270 million years ago, the therapsid reptiles began to evolve. Unlike the pelycosaurs, with their somewhat sprawling, short-legged gait, the therapsids had longer legs that were positioned further back under their bodies, which meant that they could

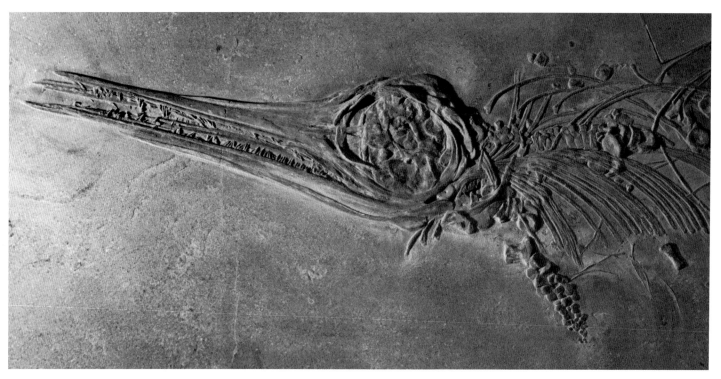

move faster with bigger strides. One of the best-known of the early therapsids was *Moschops* – still a fairly clumsy, lumbering creature, but more advanced than the pareiasaurs. About 16-ft (5-m) long, *Moschops* also had a strong skull, the roof of which was covered with 4-in (10-cm) thick bone. This feature, together with the strong neck vertebrae, suggests that moschops may

have used its head as a kind of battering ram in trials of strength with competitors at mating time.

By the start of the Triassic period, about 248 million years ago, the therapsids had evolved into many different species, the most common types of which were the plant-eating dicynodonts and the carnivorous cynodonts. Two large tusks, one on each side of the jaws,

were used to dig up plant roots, and a tough beak and horny plates in the mouths of dicynodonts ground the food up. *Lystrosaurus,* a 4-ft (1.5-m) long dicynodont, may have led a semi-aquatic existence. Many of the cynodonts had slender, almost dog-like bodies and long legs for running down prey. They also had powerful teeth of various kinds, designed for stabbing, shearing and chewing

An ichthyosaur or 'fish-lizard' (Ichthyosaurus sp.). It used its many teeth for grabbing and holding on to slippery fish prey.

Replica of a pterodactyl (Pterodactylus kochi). *This example, from the late Jurassic period, had a wingspan of 18in (46cm), each wing supported by an elongated fourth digit in the hand. Pterodactyls were carnivores, and caught their prey in their long, pointed beaks armed with many small teeth. The original fossil was found in lithographic limestone in Solnhofen, Bavaria, Germany.*

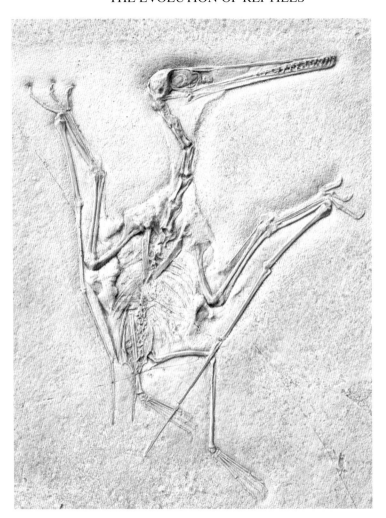

the flesh of their victims. It is possible that they could generate their own body heat, like warm-blooded birds and mammals. *Thrinaxodon* was a cynodont from the Triassic period whose fossil remains have been found in South Africa. Some cynodonts may even have had fur and whiskers. Towards the end of the Triassic period, the cynodonts gave rise to the first true mammals, which for some time co-existed with the ruling reptiles. However, they only expanded to become the dominant group we see today after the sudden and catastrophic events that heralded the end of the dinosaurs and many other types of ancient creatures.

PREHISTORIC AQUATIC REPTILES

Having successfully lived on dry land for about 80 million years, some groups of reptiles then returned to the water. This may seem an unusual route to have taken after having dominated life on land for so long, but in fact it was simply an evolutionary inevitability. The lakes, rivers and oceans were vast and varied potential habitats, abounding with new opportunities to be exploited by creatures with the necessary adaptations. Consequently, the aquatic reptiles became highly evolved to face the challenges of these new environments. The marine ichthyosaurs came to resemble modern-day dolphins, their bodies streamlined for fast swimming; instead of legs they had powerful front flippers, fins and a broad tail, and their

A dinosaur footprint in situ in north Arizona, U.S.A.

A replica of the theropod Compsognathus from the late Jurassic period, a small chicken-sized carnivorous dinosaur which fed on insects and small lizard-like creatures.

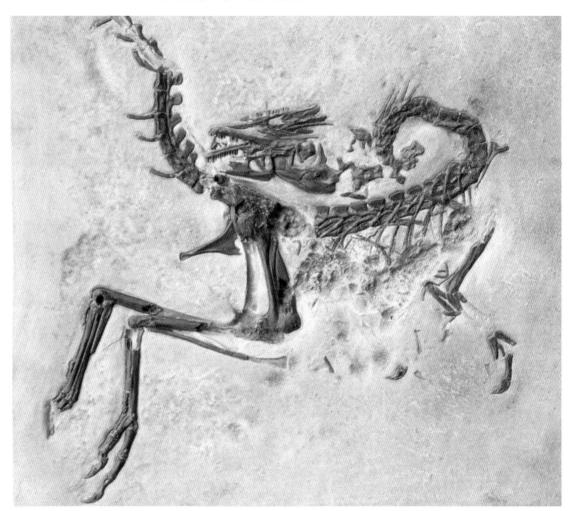

Cast of a footprint of dinosaur Chirotherium barthi, *from the Triassic period.*

RIGHT
Replica of a feathered dinosaur
(Caudipteryx)*, one of the few non-*
avian dinosaurs. Note the stomach
stones (gastroliths) in the belly.
Found in Liaoning province, north-
east China.

OPPOSITE
Upper jaw of the large meat-eating
dinosaur Tyrannosaurus rex*, which*
lived in the Cretaceous period
85–65 million years ago.

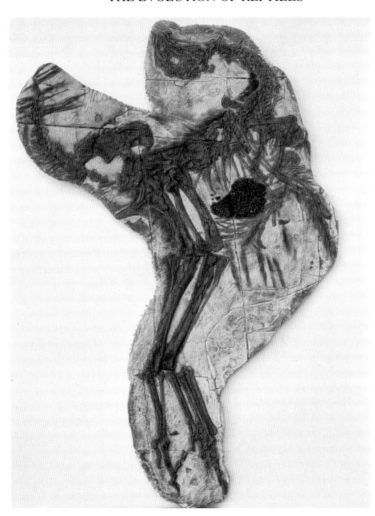

mouths were lined with rows of sharp teeth. It is possible that they hunted in packs, encircling, then gulping down shoals of fish. Because they had no legs, ichthyosaurs gave birth, like some of the sea snakes, to live young in the water. Mesosaurs were rather crocodile-like in appearance, having long, thin jaws with sharp teeth. They also had legs and long, flattened tails to help them to swim. The plesiosaurs had two pairs of well-developed flippers for swimming, while *Kronosaurus* was a short-necked plesiosaur that grew to about 39ft (12m) in length. *Elasmosaurus* had an extremely long neck and reached a length of about 42ft (13m). Rather than chasing prey, this plesiosaur probably dipped its long neck into the water to grab passing fish. Among the freshwater aquatic reptiles were giant crocodiles like *Deinosuchus*, which grew to a length of 49ft (15m), and turtle-like creatures such as *Henodus*.

CONQUEST OF THE AIR

Just as some reptiles evolved features which enabled them to exploit the lakes, rivers and oceans, so a few evolved the means to conquer the air. The first flying reptiles arose about 225 million years ago and were called pterosaurs. Unlike today's flying reptiles – that really do no more than glide a short distance – the pterosaurs could sometimes remain aloft for hours on end, soaring effortlessly over the surface of the sea to grab fish and other creatures. The wings of pterosaurs were formed from leathery skin

stretched between the fore- and hindlimbs,
rather like the wing arrangement found in
bats. It is likely that pterosaurs could achieve
flapping flight, remaining airborne for as
long as they chose to beat their wings,
twisting and turning to change direction and
even to chase flying insects. One of the best-
known pterosaurs is *Pterodactylus*, a fairly
small but manoeuvrable creature with a long
beak and short tail, which may have slept
hanging upside-down like a bat. But it was
about 75 million years ago, in the Cretaceous
period, that the real giants of the air evolved.
Quetzalcoatlus was an immense pterosaur
with a 50-ft (15-m) wingspan – far bigger
than any other flying animal as far as we
know. Some of the flying reptiles may even

have developed fur to keep their bodies warm
so that they could fly more efficiently.

THE RISE AND FALL OF THE
DINOSAURS

No account of reptiles is complete
without describing the dinosaurs. From a few
tiny, ancestral forms, the dinosaurs expanded
and multiplied to become the masters of the
earth for millions of years. Some grew to
titanic proportions, leading to almost endless
speculation as to how they could possibly
have existed. The anatomical features of
others have caused scientists to propose that
they lived in herds, with social structures and
hierarchies like those seen in some of the
herding mammals alive today, and that some

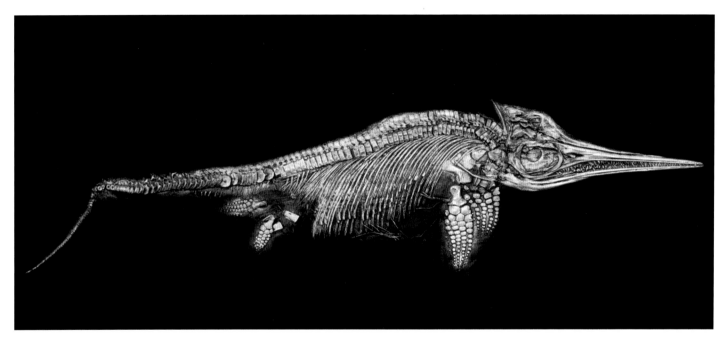

of them even possessed intelligence to match.

The story of the dinosaurs begins in the Triassic period, about 225 million years ago, at the time when a group of reptiles called the archosaurs were still alive. The early archosaurs were crocodile-like creatures like *Stagonolepis,* that spent much of their time hunting prey in the water. Later, archosaurs like *Lagosuchus,* that could run on land on two legs, developed, using a long tail to help them balance. From such reptiles the dinosaurs are believed to have evolved.

Eoraptor, a small, fast-moving carnivore was one of the first true dinosaurs, whose remains were discovered in 1992. For 160 million years or so, the relatives of such a creature would become some of the biggest, strongest and strangest animals ever to have lived.

The reason for the early success of the dinosaurs is largely due to their special limb arrangements that enabled them to stand upright and move easily and efficiently. It helped some species to outrun and catch prey, and it helped others to escape from slower-

moving enemies. Dinosaurs became adaptable, varied and versatile and in time established themselves all over the world. A few hundred years ago, a scientist called Henry Seeley proposed a new way of classifying dinosaurs by dividing them into two groups based on the structure of their hip bones. He called one group, whose hip bones were arranged like those of lizards, lizard-hipped dinosaurs. The lizard-hipped dinosaurs include the largest and also the fiercest of all dinosaurs, including four-

Ichthyosaur was a marine reptile known as a 'fish-lizard' that lived in oceans in the Mesozoic period.

Replica of a dinosaur nest with 80 million-year-old round eggs. It was found in China.

legged plant-eating giants like *Brachiosaurus* and *Argentinosaurus*, weighing 100 tons or more. Others included the terrifying carnivorous species like *Tyrannosaurus rex* and *Carcharodontosaurus* at 40ft (12m) or more in length. The second group contained the bird-hipped dinosaurs, so-called because their hip bones resembled those of birds, and

which did not evolve until after the lizard-hipped dinosaurs, even though, in time, many different kinds appeared. Some, like *Hypsilophodon*, walked only on their back legs, while others, such as *Stegosaurus*, walked on all fours. All of the bird-hipped dinosaurs were plant-eaters.

Just as the Age of Reptiles produced

many varied species adapted to widely differing habitats, from the flying pterosaurs to the aquatic ichthyosaurs, so the Age of Dinosaurs was punctuated by a huge diversity of creatures of varying shapes, sizes and lifestyles. Among the carnivorous species this is perhaps less so, for the perfect meat-eating dinosaur – a fast-moving, powerful animal

with clawed hands, strong jaws and lethal teeth – developed fairly quickly. All that was really required was to refine the model to meet the challenge of bigger or different prey, and this came mainly in the form of increased body size, stronger back legs (and the reduction of the front legs) and a heavier skull with stronger jaws and bigger teeth.

For the plant-eaters, however, evolution produced a huge parade of species with different shapes and anatomical features. The sauropods became the largest animals ever to have lived, their huge, barrel-shaped bodies supported on vast legs like tree trunks. A long neck terminated in a tiny head armed with flat, grinding teeth, and the body extended into an extremely long tail. One of them, *Seismosaurus,* probably reached a length of 160ft (49m). Many of these giant reptiles lived like modern-day elephants, having few enemies because of their huge size and roaming the landscape browsing the trees at will. Other plant-eating dinosaurs developed ornate and elaborate head crests, thick, domed

Fossil replica jaw with teeth of a Mosasaur *– a large prehistoric lizard-like reptile adapted to life in water. It used its powerful jaws to prey upon fish, turtles and molluscs.*

Fossil replica, showing skull and lower jaw of an agamid lizard from the Eocene period.

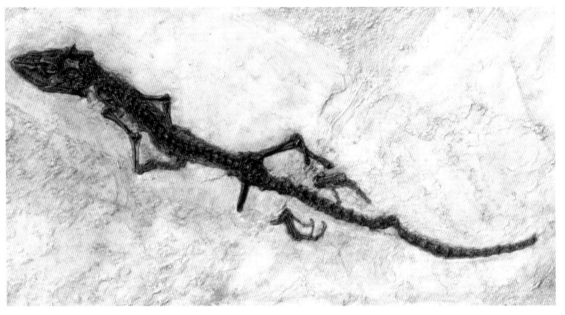

skulls or duck-like beaks. The zenith of bizarre adornments came with the triceratopians, however. Possibly as a defence against the huge predatory dinosaurs like *Tyrannosaurus rex*, as well as a means of settling territorial and mating disputes among their own kind, species such as *Triceratops* and *Styracosaurus* developed huge horns on their heads and noses and elaborate broad, bony neck shields. In many ways, triceratopians filled the niches occupied today by the rhinoceroses. Furthermore, among all this dinosaurian diversity, about 150 million

years ago, the first birds also arose from small, meat-eating dinosaurs.

From about 65 million years onward, the fossil record is suddenly devoid of evidence of dinosaurs. Missing, too, are any traces of the flying pterosaurs and many marine reptiles. Something caused the complete and sudden destruction of all these successful and flourishing reptile groups, but what? Many different theories have been proposed for the cause of this catastrophic event, but scientists now generally believe that an impact by a huge meteorite was to blame. Coinciding

with the end of the dinosaurs, a massive meteorite hit Chicxulub on Mexico's Yucatan Peninsula, an event that would have altered the earth's climate dramatically. The impact would have sent huge dust clouds into the air, blocking out the sun and plunging the planet into cold, permanent darkness. The drop in temperature would have been disastrous for many animals. The lack of sun would have prevented plants from growing, thus killing the herbivorous dinosaurs and ultimately the carnivores that fed upon them. A drop in temperature would also have killed many sea

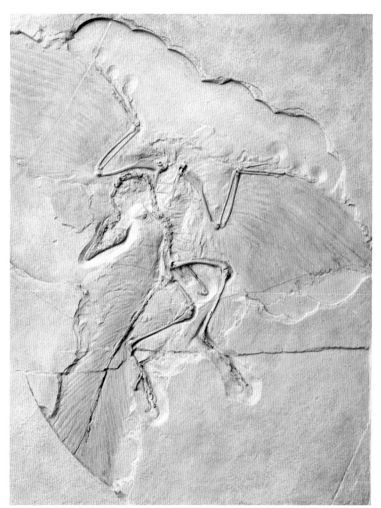

creatures, and great winds would have blown up, preventing the pterosaurs from flying, while massive earthquakes and tidal waves would have struck the earth, causing even more destruction.

Likely though this theory is, it still leaves some unanswered questions. Why, for example, did some animals, and more significantly many reptiles, survive the impact's aftermath? The crocodiles, turtles, lizards and snakes all survived, and so did the birds and the mammals. Perhaps some of the small creatures that survived were able to burrow to safety and others were able to use their warm-bloodedness to stay alive? Whatever killed the dinosaurs, it left the way clear for the mammals to inherit the earth and eventually to become the dominant life forms of today.

FAR LEFT
Replica of a specimen of the Jurassic bird-like reptile fossil, Archaeopteryx lithographica, *with feather imprints on the forelimbs and a long tail and obvious teeth. Found in lithographic limestone at Solnhofen in Bavaria.*

BELOW
Replica of the skull of Archaeopteryx lithographica, *showing teeth on both jaws.*

CHAPTER THREE
TORTOISES & TURTLES

*A giant tortoise (*Geochelone elephantopus vandenburghii*). Note the short, stout legs necessary to carry the heavy shell.*

The tortoises and turtles make up the group of reptiles known as the chelonians, or the order Chelonia or Testudines. The chelonians first made their appearance in the fossil record some 215 million years ago, when the first dinosaurs were alive but before the lizards or snakes had evolved. The chelonians are therefore among the earliest of all reptiles to have evolved, having about 295 living species split into 14 families, with some living on land and others in fresh or in sea water. Conventionally, chelonians that live in the water are usually called turtles and the rest are known as tortoises, although those that are found in fresh water are often described as terrapins. Chelonians are distributed throughout the tropical and temperate regions of the world, the only continent from which they are absent being Antarctica, where in fact no reptiles at all are to be found. Chelonians reproduce by internal fertilization, and in all species the eggs are laid on land, even if the rest of the animals' lives are spent entirely in the water.

A photograph of the green turtle (Chelonia mydas) *taken head-on.*

A turtle riding on the head of a spectacled caiman, Caiman crocodilus, *in Venezuela.*

The eastern box turtle (Terrapene carolina). Box turtles are one of the most long-lived groups of reptiles.

One of the most remarkable features of chelonians is the almost legendary longevity achieved by some species; American box turtles are known to live for up to 120 years in the wild, and in captivity tortoises have been known to survive for more than 150 years. One of the best-known instances of well-documented old age concerns the specimens collected from the Seychelles by French explorer Marion de Fresne in 1776, which were subsequently taken to the island of Mauritius in the Indian Ocean, then under the

*A European pond turtle (*Emys orbicularis*) photographed at the Maremma National Park, Italy.*

jurisdiction of the French. In 1810 the island was captured by the British during the Napoleonic Wars and the tortoises came under their care, when they became somewhat famous inhabitants of the garrison at the island's capital, Port Louis. All but one of the tortoises had died by 1918, although one survived. However, this individual met an untimely end in that same year, after 152 years in captivity. Now blind, the unfortunate reptile fell into a gun emplacement and subsequently died from its injuries. In effect, this tortoise did not die of old age, and was possibly already an adult when captured, so it is likely that it may have been about 200 years old when it finally died.

In the wild, aquatic turtles have been estimated to live for between 40 and 75 years, although accurate documentation has only been kept for individuals, such as painted turtles (*Chrysemys picta*). European pond turtles (*Emys orbicularis*), kept in captivity, have been known to live for 70 years, and a number of other species seem to have lived for 60 years or so. Marine loggerhead turtles (*Caretta caretta*) have survived for 33 years in captivity, and specific green turtles (*Chelonia mydas*) have been noted coming back to the same beach to lay their eggs for 20 years or more.

A SHELTERED LIFE

Part of this long life and durability no doubt stems from the unique way in which the majority of chelonians protect themselves from would-be predators, for they can withdraw their heads and limbs inside a tough, bony box or shell when danger threatens. The shell of a chelonian is made up of about 60 separate bones and consists of two main parts: the carapace forms the dome-like covering over the animal's back, and the flatter plastron forms the underbelly region, the two parts joined together at the sides by extensions of the plastron. In some species large scales known as scutes cover the shell, but in others the shell is covered by a leathery skin. However, there is a cost to pay for the great protection that the shell affords. The shell is not only an extremely heavy structure to carry about, but if it is to be an effective shelter for withdrawing into when the need

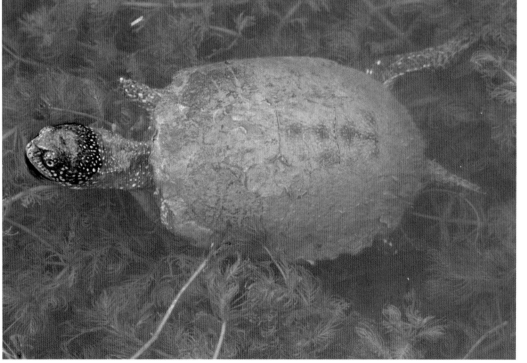

This green turtle (Chelonia mydas) is seen on a beach near a turtle-rearing facility in the Tarutao National Park, Thailand.

*This giant tortoise (*Geochelone elephantopus vandenburghii*) in the Galapagos Islands has withdrawn its head into its shell.*

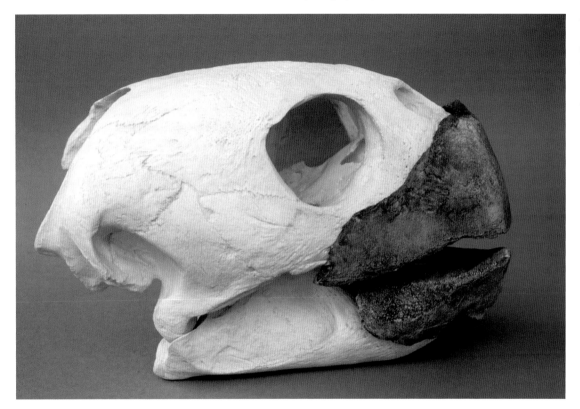

arises, then it must also be strong, broad and enveloping. For these reasons, chelonians have enjoyed only modest adventures into diversity of body form compared with some of their reptilian relatives in other groups. There are no species of flying tortoises or turtles, as there are among the lizards and snakes, and no tortoises or turtles that jump or run. Instead, chelonians have evolved to exploit successfully various terrestrial and aquatic habitats, while more or less retaining the 'standard' body plan of their ancestors. Fossils of some extinct turtles indicate that they had teeth, but all living species of chelonians have lost these and rely instead on horny jaws – although these can still be formidable weapons.

Such modifications to the body plan that do exist often involve changes in the shape and structure of the all-important shell itself. For example, in some of the more recently

evolved forms the shell has become lighter in weight due to a thinning of the bones that make it up. In the most extreme cases, such as the marine leatherback turtle (*Dermochelys coriacea*), the shell is reduced to a covering of leathery skin strengthened by small plates of bone embedded in it. Although a reduction in bone means the reptile loses some of the protection afforded by the shell, it is more than compensated for by allowing the animal to move more quickly and easily and with less expenditure of energy. In aquatic forms, the lighter shell also helps to improve buoyancy.

Aquatic chelonians (turtles and terrapins) have shells with a fairly flattened shape. This streamlining helps them as they move through the water. In the softshells – species that hide under sand or mud – the shell is often flattened even more, and is a shape seen, for example, in the Nile softshell (*Trionyx triunguis*) of African ponds, lakes and rivers and the spiny softshell (*Trionyx spiniferus*) of American creeks and ponds. Land-going tortoises tend to have high-domed shells that make them more difficult for a predator's jaws to grasp, but there are some interesting exceptions. The

pancake tortoise (*Malacochersus tornieri*) of
Kenya and Tanzania lives in rocky outcrops. It
is a small species, only about 6-in (15-cm)
long, and it can hide in small crevices in rocks
because, as its name implies, the shell is
flattened instead of domed. Interestingly, the
flattened shell also allows the tortoise to
quickly right itself should it falls over onto its
back – a manoeuvre that other species find
very difficult.

A few chelonians have yet another
adaptation of the shell. In these species, the
bones that make it up are not fixed to each
other in a fully rigid fashion. African and

American mud turtles, for example, can pull
the plastron (the lower part of the shell)
upwards, making it possible to close the shell
once the vulnerable head and limbs have
retracted inside. Movement of the plastron
allows the female freshwater Asian leaf turtle
(*Cyclemys dentata*) to more easily lay her large
eggs. The shells of many chelonians are
beautifully patterned and marked and often
have a shiny lustre – features which have
unfortunately increased the demand for their
shells as curios. Also, pieces of turtle shell,
usually known as 'tortoiseshell', have often
been used in fine decorative work such as for

inlays and making combs and other items.
Sometimes the shell patterning and colouring
also extends onto the heads and legs. For
example, the pond slider (*Pseudemys scripta*)
of the Americas has a shell marked with a
variable pattern of black and yellow rings
and lines, with similar markings on the head
and legs.

THE BIG AND THE SMALL

There is considerable variation in size among
chelonians. The largest species is the
leatherback turtle (*Dermochelys coriacea*).
Individuals average 6–7ft (1.8–2.1m) in
length from beak tip to tail end and may
weigh up to 1,000lb (450kg). In 1988, a huge
leatherback turtle was washed up dead on
Harlech beach in Wales after it had been

FAR RIGHT
*Detail of the shell of a radiated
tortoise (Geochelone radiata).*

BELOW RIGHT
*Detail of the shell pattern of the star
tortoise (Testudo elegans).*

caught up in a fishing line. It weighed an
astonishing 2,120lb (962kg). On land, the
Aldabran giant tortoise (*Geochelone
gigantea*) of the Indian Ocean islands of
Aldabra, Mauritius and the Seychelles reaches
a length of 5.7ft (1.4m) and a weight of 560lb
(254kg), while a male Aldabran giant tortoise
living on Bird Island in the Seychelles, and
curiously named Esmeralda, attained a weight
of 657lb (298kg) in 1989. Another large
species is the marine green turtle (*Chelonia
mydas*), reaching a length of over 4ft (1.2m).
Smaller than the aforementioned species, but
nevertheless of considerable size, the
aggressive alligator snapping turtle
(*Macroclemys temminckii*) of the central
U.S.A. reaches a length of 28in (72cm). The
smallest chelonians are the speckled cape
tortoise (*Homopus signatus*) and the bog
turtle (*Clemmys muhlenbergii*), which only
grow to about 4in (10cm) or so.

CHELONIAN BIOLOGY

Turtles and tortoises do not have teeth.
Instead, the jaws are equipped with horny
beaks, which in some species are quite long
and may be armed with sharp projections.
The two eyes are usually fairly large and
situated prominently on either side of the
head. Turtles and tortoises breathe through
lungs, but they use special sets of muscles to
expand them to draw in air. This is because
the ribs are fused to the rigid shell and
cannot therefore be used in the breathing
process as they are in other vertebrates.

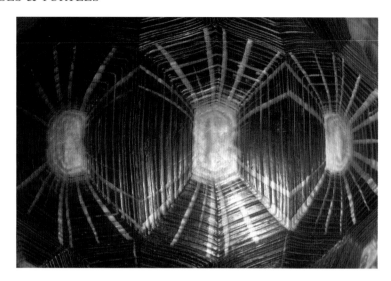

*Giant tortoise (*Testudo gigantea).

*The world's smallest tortoise, the speckled cape (*Homopus signatus*), pictured among the gazanias.*

Chelonians that live in water can also breathe through their skin, through special sacs in the cloaca and through the throat lining. Some aquatic species, such as the soft-shelled turtles, use their snorkel-like nose to breathe in air while remaining on the mud at the bottom of rivers and ponds. Turtles are capable of surviving in extremely low levels of oxygen – a useful adaptation for species that may need to stay submerged for long periods to avoid predators or when diving in search of food. Experiments have shown that the loggerhead musk turtle (*Sternotherus minor*) can live submerged almost indefinitely, provided that the water is saturated with oxygen.

All tortoises and turtles have two pairs of limbs which, in almost all species, are placed squarely one at each corner of the shell. As described on page 20, the pectoral and pelvic girdles of a chelonian, to which the limbs are

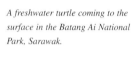

A freshwater turtle coming to the surface in the Batang Ai National Park, Sarawak.

BELOW

A green turtle showing the pattern of the scutes in the dorsal shell or carapace.

OPPOSITE

The large foreflippers of a green turtle.

fixed, are themselves connected to the inner parts of bones making up the shell. In land-going species, the scaly legs are short and stout to help bear the weight of the cumbersome and heavy shell, and the toes are also short. The slow locomotion of tortoises is the stuff of fables and legends; for example, the desert tortoise (*Gopherus agassizii*) moves along at no more than about 0.3mph (0.5 km/h).

The limbs of aquatic turtles and terrapins have longer toes, between which are stretched webs of skin that help the reptiles to 'row' through the water when swimming. Some of the marine species of turtle have even more highly-modified limbs. For example, in the leatherback turtle (*Dermochelys coriacea*), the hawksbill turtle (*Eretmochelys imbricata*), the green turtle (*Chelonia mydas*), the olive ridley turtle (*Lepidochelys olivacea*) and the loggerhead turtle (*Caretta caretta*) the forelimbs in particular have become large, flat, paddle-like structures; the foreflippers of the loggerhead turtle may easily reach a span of 9ft (2.7m). In several species the claws and scales have also been lost to help improve the streamlining. While these modifications are a necessity for creatures that spend almost their

Page 96: Image supplied by Jon Hanson\Flickr Creative Commons.

OPPOSITE
*The hawksbill turtle (*Eretmochelys imbricata*) gets its name from its hook-like, beaky jaws.*

LEFT
A leatherback turtle hauling itself out onto a beach in Trinidad.

*An eastern box turtle (*Terrapene carolina*) shooting its neck out from its shell.*

whole lives swimming endlessly in the open sea, such limbs are woefully inadequate for use on land. It is almost pitiful to watch the effort it takes for a female turtle to haul herself up a beach to lay her eggs ashore, and to return, exhausted, to the welcoming surf that will carry her to the safety of the open sea. Many freshwater turtles use their limbs for a combination of walking and swimming, but their alternating paddle-like swimming strokes cannot match the grace of the seaturtles as they glide effortlessly through the oceans with their powerful flippers.

The ribs and most of the vertebral column, or backbone, are also fused to the inner shell, with the rear part of the vertebral column extending into the tail. In some species, such as the snapping turtle (*Chelydra serpentina*) and the alligator snapping turtle (*Macroclemys temminckii*), the tail is long and extremely prominent, and extends well beyond the end of the shell, while in others, the tail is small and concealed beneath the shell. Although chelonians are somewhat limited in their lifestyles by their shells, nature has nevertheless provided them with extremely mobile necks. According to the species, the neck can be extended forward to reach vegetation growing some distance from the ground, or shot out at speed to capture unsuspecting prey. (This is one part of a chelonian that does move fast!) At the same time, the neck can be quickly contracted to draw the vulnerable head safely into the protective haven of the shell when danger

*Galapagos giant tortoises (*Geochelone elephantopus vandenburghii*), possibly about to mate.*

threatens. In most of the families of chelonians the neck bends in an up-and-down, S-shaped movement, but in the Chelidae and Pelomedusidae families the head is retracted into the shell by the neck bending in a sideways movement, giving rise to the name 'side-necked turtles' when describing these two families.

*Captive juvenile Mediterranean spur-thighed or Greek tortoises (*Testudo graeca ibera*) feeding.*

FINDING FOOD AND LIFESTYLES

Because tortoises and turtles are relatively slow-moving, their prey is usually also of the slow-moving variety. Thus creatures such as sponges, mussels, barnacles, worms, insect larvae and dead animals form the bulk of the food in most carnivorous species, while many other species are omnivorous, taking a mixture of animal and plant food. For a number of other species, including most of the tortoises that make up the family Testudinidae, vegetation is the preferred food. Quite often food is either simply snapped up and swallowed whole, or grazed off in chunks by the chelonian's horny jaws. However, instead of actively hunting for prey, a number of species have resorted to more unusual methods to obtain their food. Some simply lie camouflaged on the bottom and ambush prey as it swims past, grabbing it in their mouths. Others lure their prey by means of a form of 'fishing' or suck victims into their mouths along with a huge gulp of water. The most celebrated exponents of these last two methods are probably the alligator snapping

turtle (*Macroclemys temminckii*) and the matamata (*Chelus fimbriata*).

The alligator snapping turtle is the largest turtle in the U.S.A. It lives in rivers and lakes and has been known to reach a length of 30in (76cm) and a weight of 200lb (91kg), although it usually grows to between 20 and 25in (51 and 64cm) in length. The creature gets its name because it was once thought, wrongly, to be a cross between an alligator

and a turtle; it certainly looks rather like a hybrid, having long jaws, a long tail and a bony, elongated shell. However, the aggressive nature of the reptile is not in doubt, and the huge, sharp jaws have been known to cause serious injury to unwary human bathers who unwittingly got too close to this well-camouflaged, armoured hunter. It inhabits dark, slow waters and spends most of its time lying still on the bottom. Indeed, it

The Mediterranean turtle (Mauremys leprosa)*, surfacing in a pool in Spain.*

A matamata turtle (Chelus fimbriata)
on land beside the Rio Tefe,
Amazonas, Brazil. The large flat head
and neck are covered with many
warty protuberances and the ones on
the sides are sensitive to water
movements caused by swimming fish,
on which the turtle preys. The long
snout allows the turtle to breathe air
while virtually submerged.

spends so much of its life in this sedentary manner that algae collect on its shell, which helps to conceal the turtle even more effectively. When feeding, the alligator snapping turtle lies with its mouth wide open, revealing a red, worm-like appendage attached to its tongue. This is waved alluringly to attract unsuspecting aquatic animals that come to investigate what appears to be a possible source of food. Once within range, however, they are swiftly grabbed in

the turtle's jaws and consumed. Anything too big to be swallowed whole is first sliced up by the jaws. The alligator snapping turtle will eat practically anything it can lure towards its mouth, including fish, crustaceans, snails and even other turtles.

The matamata is a somewhat smaller turtle that lives in rivers in the northern part of South America, growing to about 16in (41cm) in length. An extremely unusual-looking reptile, it has a curious, algae-covered, rough

and ridged shell. The head is flat and almost triangular in shape and terminates in a thin, tube-like snout. Beneath the snout, the matamata has an extremely wide mouth but has no horny covering to its jaws, unlike most chelonians. It is well camouflaged by its irregularly-shaped brown shell. Lying in wait for prey on the bottom of the river, it resembles dead leaves, an illusion that is further enhanced by the fleshy flaps of skin that adorn either side of the head. The flaps are waved invitingly in the water and not only attract potential prey but also detect the presence of animals nearby, thus alerting the reptile. When a fish swims close, the matamata opens its huge mouth, creating a low pressure that sucks in the prey as well as water. The mouth then closes, leaving just a small opening for the water to escape, and the fish is swallowed.

Some species of omnivorous chelonians may eat certain types of food when they are young, then switch to others when they get older. For example, a turtle may eat snails and insects when young, but subsist mainly on plants when adult. Sometimes, the diets of males and females differ – especially when the two sexes are of different sizes.

Although chelonians seek out others of their kind for mating and egg-laying, they also congregate at other times. The painted turtle (*Chrysemys picta*) is one of several species that congregate to bask, and the green turtle (*Chelonia mydas*) and loggerhead turtle (*Caretta caretta*) are just two of several kinds

that are known to overwinter together. Many turtles and tortoises live in more or less defined territories where they feed and rest, and although they probably do not defend their territories in the same way that some other animals do, they may still try to exert dominance over other individuals. Another

interesting example of behaviour concerns the practice of mutual grooming in which some species of turtles remove algae and other small fragments from each other's shells with their mouths. Occasionally, land tortoises may share underground burrows with other reptile species in times of drought.

REPRODUCTION

Distinguishing between the sexes of turtles and tortoises is not always easy. Sometimes coloration can be used to tell them apart, although in many species the males and females are the same colour. Often the differences are small: for example, one sex

Yellow-spotted side-necked turtles (Podocnemis unifilis) in Peru.

BELOW
*Giant tortoises (*Geochelone elephantopus vandenburghii*) mating.*

BELOW RIGHT
*Angulate tortoises (*Chersina angulata*) mating.*

may have red eyes and one may have brown. In the spotted turtle (*Clemmys guttata*), the male has brown eyes and brown coloration on the chin, whereas the female has orange eyes and a yellow chin. Males of most species of chelonians have thicker tails than females, with the vent situated farther back. Males also have more concave plastrons (the underpart of the shell) so that they can more easily negotiate the arched top of the female's shell when mating. Sometimes males have longer snouts or other slight anatomical differences that separate them from females.

There are often elaborate courtship displays among chelonians, especially in the aquatic species in which the male is smaller than the female. In species where the male is bigger, such as the snapping turtles and the land-based tortoises, the niceties of courtship are often replaced by more straightforward strategies whereby the male simply overpowers the female and proceeds to mate with her. Such courtship as does exist among tortoises usually involves some head-bobbing, head-thrusting and perhaps biting on the part of the male prior to his clambering onto the back of the female's shell, while giant tortoises (*Geochelone gigantea*) may utter bellowing sounds as part of the courtship ritual. Some male pond and river turtles use their long, clawed forelimbs to touch the female's snout as part of their

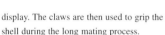

display. The claws are then used to grip the shell during the long mating process.

True to their reptilian inheritance, all species of chelonians lay eggs on land and even the highly aquatic marine turtles must leave the water at this time. For some species, the best breeding grounds – and the places where they lay their eggs – may be a great distance from their normal feeding areas, and they must sometimes swim hundreds of miles to reach their destination. The green turtle (*Chelonia mydas*) – which gets its name because its fat is green – undertakes a huge migration at breeding time. Usually, this large turtle spends its life grazing seagrass meadows off the coast of Brazil, but at breeding time it migrates unerringly to Ascension Island in the middle of the Atlantic Ocean, a distance of 1,300 miles (2100km). More remarkable still is the fact that Ascension Island is a tiny island a mere 5-miles (8-km) wide.

When the female loggerhead turtle is ready to lay her eggs she hauls herself out of the sea and up the beach, well away from the crashing swell. She then uses her foreflippers to create a depression in the sand and lies down in it. Once she is in position, she digs a hole about 16-in (41-cm) deep using her hindflippers. About 100 or so eggs are then laid in the hole, which she then covers with sand before hauling herself back down to the

RIGHT
Green turtle embryo.

FAR RIGHT
Hatching out.

OPPOSITE
*Green turtle hatchlings breaking out
from their nest site in a sandy beach.*

RIGHT
Green turtle embryo.

FAR RIGHT
Hatching out.

OPPOSITE
*Green turtle hatchlings breaking out
from their nest site in a sandy beach.*

water. Protected by the covering of sand, the baby turtles incubate for a period of about two or three months; when they are ready to hatch, the baby turtles break out of their shells and dig towards the surface. Now is the most hazardous part of their lives. Guided by a combination of high air humidity, reflected light and the sound of the crashing surf on the beach, the hatchlings make for the safety of the water as fast as they can. Sadly, many fall victim on the way to waiting predators such as seabirds and crabs, against which the tiny turtles have no defence. But a few make it safely to the sea, although even in this relative haven the hatchlings are beset by perils from aquatic hunters until they have grown substantially larger.

Sometimes, turtles nest together in huge numbers. Olive ridley turtles (*Lepidochelys olivacea*) may form nesting groups comprising over 200,000 individuals, all laying their eggs over a period of one or two days on a few miles of beach. This mass

Green turtle hatchlings head for the sea at dawn in Sarawak.

nesting is known as an 'arribada', one of the best-known being the one that occurs at Orissa, India. Such large congregations of nests have advantages, because with so many in one place, predators are bound to leave many untouched. The rare river terrapin (*Batagur baska*) and the South American river turtle (*Podocnemis expansa*) also nest en masse.

For many land-dwelling and freshwater chelonians the journey to their nest is a short one, with most species finding a suitable place to lay their eggs fairly close to where they usually live and search for food. Some chelonian species lay eggs every year, while

others lay only every two or three years. Tortoises and a few species of turtle lay hard-shelled eggs, but the eggs of marine turtles and many river turtles have soft shells. The eggs of some chelonian species, such as the matamata (*Chelus fimbriata*) and the Galapagos giant tortoise (*Geochelone elephantopus*), are round or almost round in shape. Others are elongated with rounded ends, such as the eggs of the snake-necked turtle (*Chelodina expansa*). Generally, the largest species produce the largest eggs: the female Galapagos giant tortoise produces eggs that can measure about 2.5in (6.5cm) across. Turtles that lay the largest number of eggs in a clutch (50 or upwards) produce round eggs, making it likely that this shape is the most efficient for enabling the greatest number of eggs to be packed close together when laid.

Although the larger marine turtles lay clutches consisting of 100 or more eggs (mainly as a mechanism to overcome the high mortality rate among hatchlings), many other chelonians lay between one and four eggs in each clutch. Eggs are laid in a variety of places according to the species, many marine turtles laying them in sand holes dug by the female, while others lay their eggs in the nests of other animals. Others make a nest mound from leaves and other vegetation, the spot-legged turtle (*Rhinoclemmys punctularia*) being one of several species that use rotting vegetation. Most chelonians simply lay their eggs, then leave them to their

*A matamata turtle (*Chelus fimbriata*) on land beside the Rio Tefe, Amazonas, Brazil.*

BELOW and OPPOSITE
*Marsh terrapins (*Pelomedusa
subrufa*).*

fate, but the Burmese brown tortoise
(*Geochelone emys*) shows a degree of
parental concern, remaining with the eggs for
some time after egg-laying and defending the
nest from intruders. Once laid, the eggs

undergo their incubation period, which can
last for about eight weeks in species
living in temperate climates, but may extend
to 16 weeks or even longer in tropical-
dwelling species.

TORTOISE AND TURTLE FAMILIES

The order Chelonia is divided into two
suborders and 13 families, although some
authorities recognize more. Several of the
families consist of only one living member.
One suborder, the Pleurodira, contains the
side-necked turtles. As mentioned previously,
these retract their heads into their shells by
bending the neck sideways. There are two
families in the Pleurodira, the Chelidae and
the Pelomedusidae. The other order, the
Cryptodira, contains the other 11 families.
Members of this suborder retract their heads
into their shells using an up-and-down, S-
shaped movement. Many of the tortoise and
turtle families contain members whose future
is at risk, mainly due to pressures caused by
hunting or the destruction of habitat.

FAMILY CHELIDAE

The family Chelidae contains about 50
species of side-necked turtles found in rivers
and marshes in tropical and temperate South
America, Australia and New Guinea. They are
more advanced than their relatives in the
family Pelomedusidae and consist of
carnivorous and omnivorous species. The
largest species in the family is the giant
snake-necked turtle (*Chelodina expansa*) that
grows to a length of 19in (48cm). The family
also includes the unusual-looking matamata
(*Chelus fimbriata*) of South America
described on page 102. The Murray river
turtle (*Emydura macquarrii*) is a well-known

*Members of the species
Podocnemididae, some sunbathing
while others are still emerging from
a shrinking pool.*

species that lives in the south-east of
Australia, where it inhabits streams. About
12-in (30.5-cm) long, this is an active turtle
that eats vegetation, tadpoles and frogs. As it
grows, so its carapace changes shape: when
first hatched, the young have almost circular
carapaces but by the time they are juveniles,
the carapaces are broadest at the back; by the
time they are adult, the carapace is more or
less oval.

Conservation status: three species are classed
as Critically Endangered; seven are
Endangered; three are Vulnerable.

FAMILY PELOMEDUSIDAE
These turtles live in fresh water in parts of
tropical Africa, Madagascar and South
America east of the Andes Mountains. The
family includes both herbivorous and
omnivorous species, of which there are about

26. The largest member of the family is the
Arrau river turtle (*Podocnemis expansa*); in
fact, this reptile is the largest of all the side-
necked turtles and can grow to 35in (89cm) in
length and attain a weight of over 100lb
(45kg). The female can be distinguished from
the male due to the former's wide, flat shell
and larger size. Adult Arrau river turtles eat
plant material only. At breeding time, huge
numbers of females congregate then travel in
large numbers to lay their eggs at suitable nest
sites, usually sandbanks. Here, as many as
100 soft-shelled eggs are laid at night before
the females return to their feeding grounds.
Like their relatives, the marine turtles, the
newly-hatched Arrau river turtles (measuring
about 2in (5cm) face a hazardous life, with
many falling victim to waiting predators.
Only a tiny percentage of the hatchlings make
iit to adulthood.

In some classification systems, certain
members of the family Pelomedusidae have
been placed in a new family, the
Podocnemididae. Under this alternative
system, species found in Africa south of the
Sahara, Madagascar and the Seychelles are
retained within the original family
Pelomedusidae, and are called African side-
necked turtles. The members of the family
Podocnemididae are distributed in tropical
South America and western parts of
Madagascar, and include the American side-
necked river turtles and the Madagascan big-
headed turtle (*Erymnochelys
madagascariensis*).

*The chicken turtle (*Deirochelys reticularia*) with water lettuce (*Pistia stratiotes*) on its back.*

*The eastern box turtle (*Terrapene carolina*).*

Conservation status: two species are Endangered; six are Vulnerable.

FAMILY EMYDIDAE

Containing over 100 species, this is the largest family of chelonians. It includes species that are fully aquatic as well as some that are semi-aquatic and even terrestrial. Overall, the food preferences of the group are equally varied, most members being omnivorous. Most emydid turtles have webbed hindfeet that are clearly adapted for swimming. In general, the family is distributed in many parts of the northern hemisphere, with a few species reaching the southern hemisphere. One subfamily is found in tropical and subtropical Asia, North Africa, southern Europe and the tropical Americas.

The other subfamily is to be found in temperate parts of North America, Europe, western Asia, north-west Africa and Argentina. Depending on the species, the family inhabits terrestrial sites, bogs, marshes, rivers, lakes and other wetlands, estuaries and coastal habitats.

Some well-known species include the highly aquatic pond slider (*Pseudemys scripta*) of the U.S.A., Central America and South America. When basking in the sun, pond sliders often choose floating logs, and sometimes several of them will bask together, lying on top of one another. Young pond sliders feed on insects, tadpoles and other small animals, but subsist mainly on plants as they mature. They are popular as pets. The eastern box turtle (*Terrapene carolina*) of the U.S.A. is far less likely to be found in water. Its food consists of slugs, worms and fruit, but it also seems to eat some species of fungi that are poisonous to human beings. After hibernating, eastern box turtles perform drawn-out courtship rituals. The beautifully-marked false map turtle (*Graptemys pseudogeographica*) is found in well-vegetated freshwater habitats in the U.S.A. Males are smaller than females and have enlarged claws on their forelimbs, which are used to drum against the female's snout during the courtship ritual to entice her to mate. The female may lay up to three clutches of eggs in a single season.

The diamondback terrapin (*Malaclemys terrapin*) is the only North American member of this family that is adapted for both fresh and brackish water. It is found on the Atlantic and Gulf coasts of the U.S.A., where it frequents saltmarshes and estuaries. About 5–9-in (13–23-cm) long, this stout little terrapin is a strong swimmer with powerful, well-built hindlimbs. By day, it usually feeds on snails, worms and other small creatures that it finds in the mud of tidal marshes and flats, but it also takes occasional plant material. When night comes, the terrapin digs itself into the soft mud, even hibernating in this fashion. (This applies to those in the northern part of their range.) The batagur

A giant tortoise (Geochelone elephantopus vandenburghii) *wallowing in mud.*

Giant tortoises in temporary pools on the floor of the Alcedo Crater, Isabela, Galapagos Islands.

*The Mediterranean spur-thighed or Greek tortoise (*Testudo graeca ibera*), one of the most popular of all pet reptiles.*

OPPOSITE
The geometric tortoise
*(*Psammobates geometricus*),*
photographed at Gordon's Bay,
Western Cape, South Africa. This is
a rare, endangered species.

LEFT
*The tent tortoise (*Psammobates*
tentorius*), showing the*
characteristic shape of the shell.

(*Batagur baska*) is an Asian emydid that is also found in brackish water, sometimes even venturing into the sea.

In the emydids, size range is from about 4in (10cm) in the case of the bog turtle (*Clemmys muhlenbergii*) to about 31.5in (80cm) in the Malaysian giant turtle (*Orlitia borneensis*).

Some taxonomists place certain members of the large family Emydidae into a new one,

the Geoemydidae. About 60 or so species are included in this alternative classification, such as the Eurasian pond and river turtles and the Neotropical wood turtles. They are distributed in tropical and subtropical Asia, southern Europe, northern Africa and tropical America.

Conservation status: 13 species are Critically Endangered; 24 are Endangered; 17 are Vulnerable.

FAMILY TESTUDINIDAE

The 47 or so species in this family comprise the land tortoises. All are strictly terrestrial and mainly herbivorous, with thick, stumpy legs. The hindlegs somewhat resemble those of elephants, while the front are heavily scaled. When danger threatens, the tortoises can pull their limbs and heads completely inside their shells, with just the soles of the hindfeet, tails and scaly fronts of the

*A radiated tortoise (*Geochelone radiata*) in Madagascar.*

forelimbs exposed. Members of the family are located in North and South America, Africa, Europe and Asia. Most testudinids have highly-domed shells. A great range of sizes exists among testudinids, the smallest species being the speckled cape tortoise (*Homopus signatus*) at only 4in (10cm) in length, while the mightiest member of the family, and indeed the biggest of all chelonians is the Aldabran giant tortoise (*Geochelone gigantea*) at 5.7-ft (1.7-m) long.

The Galapagos giant tortoise (*Geochelone elephantopus*) is also huge, measuring 4ft (1.2m) in length. Scattered across the various islands of the Galapagos and isolated because they are strictly terrestrial, more than a dozen subspecies of the Galapagos tortoise have evolved, each

*A leopard tortoise (*Testudo pardalis*), so-called due to its shell markings.*

adapted slightly differently to cope with the varying conditions on each island. For example, some species have a so-called saddleback shell that is shaped in such a way that the tortoise can lift its head into a more upright position to graze on higher-growing vegetation. Galapagos tortoises eat many kinds of vegetation, and most feeding takes place in the more fertile, upland areas of the islands. Mating can occur at any time of the year, and after copulation the females move down to the lowland areas to lay their eggs in pits. First the female urinates on the soil to soften it, then she digs a hole into which she deposits up to 17 eggs. She then covers the excavation with the soil she has dug out, leaving it to harden in the sun. Once the eggs have hatched, the young tortoises must dig themselves out of the egg cavity.

Schweigger's hingeback tortoise (*Kinixys erosa*) is one of several *Kinixys* species with an unusual modification to its carapace. A hinge, located at the junction of the second and third back plates, allows the shell to be lowered at this point to protect the back of the body if attacked. This tortoise hides away in vegetation when not feeding.

The gopher tortoise (*Gopherus polyphemus*) inhabits sandy places in the southern U.S.A. Its heavily-scaled front legs are flattened to aid digging, for this species prefers to spend much of its time under the ground in tunnels it digs itself, which can be very long at over 45ft (14m). The end of the tunnel widens out to form a chamber in which the tortoise hides up, remaining comfortably in an environment of fairly constant temperature and humidity. So desirable is this refuge that other small creatures often come to share it. The tortoise only leaves its tunnel to graze on vegetation.

The 6-in (15-cm) long spur-thighed or Greek tortoise (*Testudo graeca*) is a native of northern Africa, southern Europe and the Middle East, where it inhabits fields, farmland and forests. The shell is moderately domed in this herbivorous species, and there is a small spur present on the thigh region of each front leg. Females tend to be bigger than males. This is one of the best-known of all reptiles, for it is commonly kept as a pet. Unfortunately, although it is relatively undemanding to maintain, it must hibernate in winter, when most deaths occur due to incorrect conditions having been provided for this vital part of the tortoise's life. Once, these, as well as some other 'pet species' like Hermann's tortoise (*Testudo hermannii*), were collected and imported from the wild. However, numbers fell to dangerous levels, and now individuals supplied as pets are usually from specially-bred, captive stock.

Conservation status: one species Critically Endangered; seven species Endangered; 15 species Vulnerable.

FAMILY CHELYDRIDAE
The snapping turtles, as this family is known, consist of just two species, both being large, highly predatory reptiles with huge heads and strong jaws. The shells are drably coloured to help the turtles remain concealed at the bottom of their aquatic habitat. (Their unusual feeding methods have been described on page 100 et seq.) The snapping turtle (*Chelydra serpentina*) ranges from southern Canada to northern South America and is found in lakes, rivers and marshes where it feeds on all kinds of aquatic animals from fish to birds. The larger alligator snapping turtle (*Macroclemys temminckii*) is found in rivers and lakes in the U.S.A., the shell of which is highly ridged and roughly textured, helping to break up the animal's outline so that it cannot be detected by potential prey. The head and neck, which cannot be retracted, are also nobbly and rough-textured.

Conservation status: the alligator snapping turtle is Vulnerable.

FAMILY KINOSTERNIDAE
The 22 species of mud and musk turtles form the family Kinosternidae, all being essentially aquatic creatures living in North and Central America and northern South America. They range in size up to about 10.5in (27cm) in the case of the scorpion mud turtle (*Kinosternon scorpioides*). Mud and musk turtles are omnivorous, with a diet that includes invertebrates such as worms, molluscs and crustaceans as well as fish and plants. The name 'musk turtle' derives from the fact that the reptiles give off an offensive

OPPOSITE
*The angulate tortoise (*Chersina
angulata*).

odour from scent glands on the skin when disturbed or threatened.

Such is the power of the odour that the common musk turtle (*Sternotherus odoratus*) of the U.S.A. is also known by its other common name of 'stinkpot'. This turtle rarely leaves the safety of its aquatic environment, but can sometimes be seen lying on branches overhanging water. Food is a mixture of insects, molluscs, fish and vegetation, also carrion.

Conservation status: four species are Vulnerable.

FAMILY STAUROTYPIDAE
Most taxonomists include the three species of the Mexican musk turtles within the family Kinosternidae. But other researchers, having noted differences in the chromosomes, regard them as distinct enough from the Kinosternidae to warrant elevation to full

RIGHT and OPPOSITE
The female leatherback turtle
(Dermochelys coriacea) *sheds tears as she comes ashore to lay her eggs at night.*

family status as the Staurotypidae. Mexican musk turtles are found in fresh water in southern Mexico south to Honduras. They are mainly carnivorous and all have large heads and carapaces, with three keels running the length of the carapace. Their plastrons are small and narrow, cruciform in shape and have seven or eight scutes. The three members of the family are the narrow-bridged musk turtle (*Claudius angustatus*), the Chiapas cross-breasted turtle or Pacific coast giant musk turtle (*Staurotypus salvinii*) and the Mexican cross-breasted turtle or Mexican giant musk turtle (*Staurotypus triporcatus*). The plastron of the narrow-bridged musk turtle has seven bones, which is unlike any other turtle, another

unique feature being the presence of two cusps on the turtle's upper jaw. The other two species are the largest in the family; the Pacific coast giant musk turtle can reach a length of 10in (25cm), while the Mexican giant musk turtle grows to almost 16in (41cm).

FAMILY CARETTOCHELYIDAE
Fossil evidence shows us that the family Carettochelyidae was once widespread, distributed in America, Asia and Europe. There is only one species living today, however, and it has a restricted distribution in southern New Guinea and the northernmost part of Australia. The living representative of

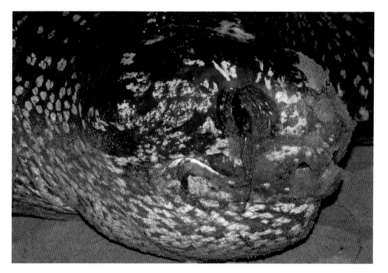

this family is the New Guinea plateless river turtle (*Carettochelys insculpta*), an 18-in (46-cm) long reptile found in rivers and lakes. It feeds on crustaceans and is well equipped for a life spent in water, for its forelimbs are modified into long, paddle-like structures though it retains two claws. Two other distinguishing features give the turtle its other common name of pig-nosed soft-shell turtle: the snout is fleshy and elongated and resembles the snout of a pig, and there is a covering of soft skin on the shell. The reptile lays between 15 and 20 eggs in a clutch, hiding them in a nest in a sandbank.

Conservation status: the New Guinea plateless river turtle is classed as Vulnerable.

FAMILY PLATYSTERNIDAE
This is another family containing only a single species. The sole member of the family is the big-headed turtle (*Platysternon megacephalum*) of Burma, Thailand and China, and it is found in mountain streams. The big-headed turtle is aptly named: although it is a fairly small species – about 7in (18cm) in length – the head is disproportionately large and nearly half the width of the carapace. The head is too big to be retracted inside the carapace, which has a slightly concave shape at the front to allow the head to be raised up. The big-headed turtle is active both day and night and is an exceptionally good climber, crawling over rocks and low vegetation in its search for food.

Conservation status: the big-headed turtle is classed as Endangered.

FAMILY DERMATEMYDIDAE

Once, this family ranged over parts of Europe, Africa and North and Central America. Today, however, there is only one living member of the family, which is found in rivers and lakes in parts of Mexico as far down as Honduras in Central America. The Central American river turtle (*Dermatemys mawii*) is about 18-in (46-cm) long, with a smooth, streamlined shell. The head is small and has a tubular pointed snout bearing large nostrils. Adult males can be distinguished by a yellow patch on the head, while females and juveniles have greyish heads. The Central

American river turtle is highly aquatic, rarely venturing onto dry land, and can remain submerged for long periods. This reptile has large webbed feet to help it swim, and it prefers to bask by floating on the water surface rather than clambering out onto the bank. It is mainly herbivorous and feeds on aquatic plants, leaves and fallen fruits. In the past, this turtle was extensively hunted for its meat and although now protected by law there is concern for its future.

Conservation status: the Central American river turtle is Endangered.

FAMILY DERMOCHELYIDAE

The family Dermochelyidae is today

RIGHT
Underside of a baby loggerhead turtle, showing the arrangement of the scutes in the lower shell or plastron.

FAR RIGHT and OPPOSITE
Green turtle (Chelonia mydas).

RIGHT
Underside of a baby loggerhead turtle, showing the arrangement of the scutes in the lower shell or plastron.

FAR RIGHT and OPPOSITE
*Green turtle (*Chelonia mydas*).*

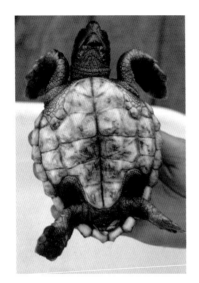

represented by a single species, the rare leatherback turtle (*Dermochelys coriacea*). This turtle, the largest of all the chelonians, typically measures 6–7ft (1.8–2.1m) in length and may weigh up to 1,000lb (454kg). The leatherback turtle derives its name from the appearance of its shell, which is covered by an oily skin and resembles hardened rubber. A series of prominent longitudinal ridges run along the length of both the upper and the lower parts of the shell. The forelimbs are modified into broad flippers and enable the turtle to range widely through the oceans of the world. It is found mainly in tropical waters but it also ventures into temperate and even subarctic conditiions. It has the unusual

Green turtle, photographed at the Tarutao National Park, Thailand.

ability of being able to keep its body temperature a few degrees above that of the surrounding sea water – a factor that helps it to survive in cold seas. The leatherback turtle has weak jaws compared with many other turtles and is mainly restricted to a diet of jellyfish and other small marine animals.

Conservation status: the leatherback turtle is classed as Critically Endangered.

FAMILY CHELONIIDAE

There are six species of turtle in this family, which is distributed in tropical, subtropical and temperate oceans. Most are under threat. All the members of this family have non-retractile heads and limbs. The forelimbs are modified to form large, flattened paddles, and the turtles swim by moving them in up-and-down motions similar to a bird's wingbeats. Because the six species in the family have overlapping ranges, they exploit different niches to avoid competing with one another. Most species are carnivorous, feeding on a range of marine animals such as fish, crustaceans, sea urchins and jellyfish. However, the green turtle (*Chelonia mydas*) grazes on seagrasses and is adapted for this diet by having serrated jaws. All of the turtles in this family must come ashore to lay their eggs, and between 80 and 200 eggs are laid in multiple clutches according to the species.

The loggerhead turtle (*Caretta caretta*) is the largest turtle in the family at 3.3ft (1.01m) or more in length. Found in temperate and

A green turtle to which remora fish have attached themselves with suckers. The spiny part of their dorsal fin is modified into a flat oval sucking plate, which the remoras use to hitch a ride on sharks, rays, turtles or other fish. They scavenge on scraps of food discarded by their hosts.

Close-up of the eye of a green turtle, showing the surrounding plates.

tropical regions of the Pacific, Atlantic and Indian Oceans, it has a large, wide head armed with strong jaws for crushing prey such as hard-shelled molluscs and   crabs. Breeding normally takes place every other year.

The green turtle is found worldwide in warm seas and undertakes long migrations to breed and lay its eggs (see page 105). Male green turtles have longer, narrower carapaces than females. They also have slightly longer claws to help them grip the female when mating. The green turtle feeds predominantly on seagrasses and seaweeds, plucking and grazing the plants with their serrated jaws. In company with other marine turtles, the green turtle's numbers have suffered severely due to hunting and egg-collecting. Turtles are also highly vulnerable to becoming trapped in fishing nets, which usually results in their death. The related, but slightly smaller, flatback turtle (*Natator depressus*) is distributed around the coast of northern Australia.

The olive ridley turtle (*Lepidochelys olivacea*) is a smallish species at 25in (63.5cm) in length and is found in tropical Pacific, South Atlantic and Indian Oceans. It eats a wide variety of marine animals, including crustaceans such as shrimp and crabs, jellyfish, molluscs and fish; all are easily dealt with by the turtle's strong jaws. Its close relative is Kemp's ridley turtle (*Lepidochelys kempii*), found in the Atlantic.

The final member of the family is the hawksbill turtle (*Eretmochelys imbricata*) that ranges throughout the tropical Caribbean Sea and Atlantic, Pacific and Indian Oceans. The unusual serrated carapace of the hawksbill provides high-quality 'tortoiseshell' and has caused the species to become endangered, although conservation measures such as hunting bans and import controls have helped reduce the decimation. The hawksbill has a tapering head which it uses like a pair of forceps to search into rock crevices and reefs for molluscs and crustaceans.

Conservation status: the hawksbill and Kemp's ridley turtles are Critically Endangered; the rest are Endangered, except for the flatback turtle, which is Vulnerable.

FAMILY TRIONYCHIDAE
There are about 25 species in the family Trionychidae, also known as the family of softshell turtles. The family is widespread in temperate and tropical North America, Africa, Asia and Indo-Australia. Most species are inhabitants of fresh water, but the giant softshell (*Pelochelys bibroni*) is found in brackish water as well as the sea, though most species also move about on land from time to time. Members of the family are mainly carnivorous but a few are omnivorous. They are characterized by their flattened, more or less pancake-shaped shells, which lack bony plates and are covered instead by leathery skin. The neck is long, retractable and mobile

*A baby Kemp's ridley turtle
(Lepidochelys kempii) emerging
from the sand in Santa Rosa
National Park, Costa Rica.*

RIGHT and OPPOSITE
*Hawksbill turtle (*Eretmochelys
imbricata*).*

The European pond terrapin (Emys orbicularis) has been singled out for population study in Italy.

and the limbs are paddle-like with three claws on each foot. The snout forms an elongated proboscis.

The spiny softshell (*Trionyx spiniferus*) is found in rivers and ponds in Canada and the U.S.A. The shell is round, dull-yellow in colour and marked with dark spots. Conical protuberances on the front of the shell are the

reason for the animal's common name. Spiny softshells are highly aquatic and feed on crawfish, crustaceans and occasional plants. The Nile softshell (*Trionyx triunguis*) grows to about 3ft (0.9m) in length and can weigh as much as 100lb (45kg). Found in lakes, ponds and rivers from Egypt to Senegal, the Nile softshell is often hunted for food.

The narrow-headed or Indian softshell (*Chitra indica*) grows to about 3ft (0.9m) in length and has a smooth broad shell and

flipper-like limbs. The head is unusually elongated and narrow and the eyes are situated well forward near the snout. The narrow-headed softshell is found in rivers, where it feeds mainly on molluscs and fish.

Conservation status: four species are Critically Endangered; five are Endangered; six are Vulnerable.

OPPOSITE RIGHT
*A Florida softshell turtle (*Trionyx
ferox*). Its long nose is used as a
kind of breathing snorkel.*

LEFT
*A souvenir stall with endangered
turtles, puffer fish, armadillos and
shells outside Pangandaran National
Park, Java.*

CHAPTER FOUR
LIZARDS

RIGHT
*Parson's chameleon (*Calumma
parsonii)*. Detail of the eye. Most
lizards have good eyesight.*

OPPOSITE
*Land iguana (*Conolophus
subcristatus)*. These iguanas live in
the arid parts of the Galapagos
archipelago, and feed on opuntia
cacti.*

Lizards are the most numerous of all the
reptiles in terms of numbers of species.
Many lizards have bolder, more active natures
than other reptiles, which means that they are
more frequently encountered by human
beings. Some of the smaller species of lizards
are also popular because they make
interesting and relatively undemanding pets.
For these reasons, they are the animals we
most often associate with the word 'reptile'.
Lizards make up the suborder Sauria or
Lacertilia in the order Squamata, that also
contains the snakes. There are about 4,560
species of lizards living today, but like other
reptile groups their classification has been
reviewed in the light of new evidence
provided by recent DNA analysis. The first
true lizards appeared on Earth about 190
million years ago.

Overall, the lizards are wide-ranging and
highly successful animals, being found in
almost all parts of the world up to elevations
of about 16,500ft (5000m). However, cold
climatic conditions limit their northern
distribution to southern Canada on the
American continent. Neither are they found in

northern Eurasia, although at least one species, the viviparous lizard (*Lacerta vivipara*), is found in Norway above the Arctic Circle. In the southern hemisphere, lizards are found down to southern South America and New Zealand but do not extend to Antarctica. Throughout the world, lizards have evolved a huge variety of lifestyles. Most live on land, where they are to be found in trees or on or under the ground, although a few specialized types are adapted to an aquatic life. Many are also active by day. Such diversity means that among the different species of lizards there is a bewildering array of shapes, sizes, colours and other adaptations, all designed to make them successful in their chosen ways of life.

Lizards vary greatly in size, the smallest species being the jaragua lizard or dwarf gecko (*Sphaerodactylus ariasae*), only discovered in 2001 on a Caribbean island off the Dominican Republic; it is a mere 0.6-in (16-mm) long – small enough to curl up on a dime. The largest of all living lizards is the Komodo dragon (*Varanus komodoensis*), a type of monitor lizard found on some of the islands in Indonesia, which can grow to over 10ft (3m) in length. It has a deservedly fearsome reputation and has even been known to eat humans. Many lizards are drably marked with green and brown coloration to help them remain concealed on the ground or in their tree homes, but other species are highly coloured or boldly marked and often adorned with bizarre spikes, horns, crests and other appendages. Such colours help to emphasize the fact that many species of lizards have good eyesight and are active

*A Komodo dragon (*Varanus komodoensis) *feeding on a goat on Komodo Island, Indonesia. It is the largest of all living lizards.*

by day when such adornments are at their most effective.

Variations on a Theme

Most lizards are instantly recognizable as such, even though there is great variation within the suborder. Many species have a typically slender, flexible body and a long, whip-like tail. The head is often a blunt wedge shape and tapers towards the nose. The long fore- and hindlimbs each terminate in five clawed digits. They are designed to enable the lizard to move about on all fours, using a symmetrical gait that causes the body to undulate from side to side as the reptile progresses. Such a description could also be used for some of the earliest types of reptiles that arose over 300 million years ago, demonstrating that the basic body plan was successful from an early stage. Having said that, a huge number of species have deviated

141

RIGHT
A *Komodo dragon (*Varanus komodoensis) *on the island of Rincha, Indonesia.*

OPPOSITE
*The common lizard (*Lacerta vivipara) *is widely distributed, from the Arctic circle down through Asia.*

RIGHT
*Slow-worm (*Anguis fragilis*). This is
a member of the lizard order, despite
its limbless, snake-like appearance.*

RIGHT
*Slow-worm (*Anguis fragilis*). This is
a member of the lizard order, despite
its limbless, snake-like appearance.*

OPPOSITE
*The ring-tailed dragon (*Ctenophorus
caudicinctus*), photographed in
Northern Territory, Australia. It is
holding its body off the ground to
avoid getting too hot.*

bodies are flattened sideways, probably to
give them more stability as they move
through foliage. The aptly named flat lizard
(*Platysaurus intermedius*) of South Africa
has a body that is flattened from top to
bottom, which means that it can squeeze into
narrow cracks among rocks to hide from
enemies. Another exponent of this technique
is the imperial flat lizard (*Platysaurus
imperator*). Once inside the safety of its
rocky crevice, the lizard inflates its flattened
body with air, wedging itself into its
hideaway and making it virtually impossible
for a predator to remove it.

Many species of lizards inhabit dry, open
plains and deserts. There is often little cover
in these environments, and movements need
to be quick – not only to avoid the extreme
heat but also because the less time spent out
in the open the less chance there is of being
seen by a predator. Therefore lizards such as
Gould's monitor (*Varanus gouldii*) have
strong, stout bodies and long limbs.

The strand racerunner (*Cnemidophorus
lemniscatus*) is another expert athelete,
sometimes running on its two back legs to
gain extra speed. Sometimes lizards use their
limbs in other ways to avoid the heat; in hot
deserts, many species adopt special stances
and other behavioural techniques to avoid
overheating. Some species, such as desert
chameleons, straighten their legs so that they
can distance their body as far away from the
ground as possible – a method known as
stilting. Another technique adopted by
various species of lizards is to alternately lift
pairs of diagonally opposing legs off the hot
sand so that overall contact is thus reduced.

from it in order to fit their chosen niches. For
example, members of several families have
lost some or all of their limbs altogether, or
simply have vestigial scaly flaps instead of
limbs. Such species usually lead a burrowing
life, having followed a similar evolutionary
path to the one taken by the worm-lizards
(another suborder of reptiles, the
Amphisbaenia, within the order Squamata),

which have also dispensed with limbs to make
the task of living underground easier.

Many lizards that spend much of their
life in the trees, such as iguanas and anoles
(family Iguanidae), have long, slender bodies
and longish legs, features which help them to
stretch from one branch to another when they
are clambering among trees. The chameleons
are also specialist tree-climbers, and their

LIZARDS

Where vegetation is to be found growing in arid, hot environments, many lizards simply climb up it to get as far away from the heat of the sand as possible. Some species, like the bearded dragon (*Pogona barbata*) of Australia, use this method during the hottest part of the day, then return to the ground as the temperature cools.

The tail, so long and distinctive in many lizards, is stumpy and reduced in others. The spiny-tailed skink (*Egernia stokesii*) of the arid regions of Australia has a short, flattened, rounded tail covered with spiny outgrowths. The leaf-tailed gecko (*Uroplatus fimbriatus*), which lives in the forests of Madagascar, has a tail which is shaped like a short spatula and, like the rest of the body, is mottled in colours of grey, white and brown that help it to remain invisible on tree bark. The broad, stumpy tail of the Gila monster (*Heloderma suspectum*) of the arid southern U.S.A. and Mexico can be used to store fat during periods of food shortage. In climbing lizards, in particular, the long tail helps provide balance when clambering about among the treetops. In many species the tail is also prehensile, acting as an extra limb when wrapped around branches. The marine iguana (*Amblyrhynchus cristatus*) of the Galapagos Islands spends most of its life diving under water to graze seaweed from the rocks, its flattened tail acting as a useful aid to swimming. The large and powerful Soa-soa

A central bearded dragon lizard (Pogona vitticeps) *near Mungeranie, South Australia.*

water dragon (*Hydrosaurus amboinensis*) lives in rainforests in parts of South-East Asia such as New Guinea and the Moluccas. Despite its size – reaching a length of about 3.7ft (1.1m) – and somewhat fearsome appearance, it feeds on plants and insects. It can run well on its back legs, but also has a flattened tail and is an excellent swimmer.

Despite its undoubted usefulness, many lizards are prepared to sacrifice their tail in the event of a potentially life-threatening encounter with an enemy (see page 57). Should a lizard be confronted by a predator, it may wave its tail invitingly, causing the enemy to shift its focus from the lizard's vulnerable head to the more expendable tail. If the predator grabs the tail, special bones allow it to immediately fracture and the tail detaches, allowing the lizard to make an escape. In time, the lizard grows a new tail, but it is rather inferior to the original one. Nearly three-quarters of all lizard families have at least some members that can lose a tail by autotomy (as this process is known), but the feature seems to be absent in the chameleons, the beaded lizards, the monitors, the xenosaurs and the Bornean earless lizard (*Lanthanotus borneensis*).

Many tree-climbing species have long claws to help them grip tree bark. The fore- and hindlimbs of the tree-dwelling chameleons are arranged in such a way that they close around a branch like a pair of pincers, with two toes on one side and three on the other. The geckos are superbly agile climbers, with special ridged pads and thousands of minute hair-like structures on the bases of their broad toes which help to increase the area in contact with surfaces, enabling them to cling upside-down on ceilings. In some species of geckos, the scales are even present on the underside of their tails to enable them to get an even better grip on tree bark and other surfaces.

Webbed feet are usually an adaptation for an aquatic life, but the web-foot gecko (*Palmatogecko rungei*) of the Namib Desert in south-west Africa rarely sees any water – certainly never enough to swim in. Instead, it uses its webbed feet to spread its weight as it clambers over the soft sand. It also uses its feet to dig burrows so that it can shelter from the searing sun and from predators. Kuhl's gecko (*Ptychozoon kuhlii*) is a 6-in (15-cm) long gecko found in the forests of South-East Asia, Indonesia and Borneo. It has fringes of skin along the sides of its head, body and tail and, like the web-foot gecko described above, also has webbed feet. But instead of using these to help it walk, it uses them to help it fly! Kuhl's gecko can glide from tree to tree using the fringes along its body which, together with the webs of skin between the

LEFT
*Leaf-tailed gecko (*Uroplatus fimbriatus*). This is a flat-bodied species, whose body shape and coloration help to camouflage it.*

FAR LEFT
*Forest gecko (*Thecadactylus sp.*). The underside of the gecko's foot, showing ridged pads that help it to grip smooth surfaces.*

toes, act as a kind of parachute. The
fringes serve another useful purpose: when
the gecko is hiding on a tree branch, it
presses them against the surface of the bark
to help break up its outline and reduce the
size of the shadow cast by its body, making it
very hard to see.

The flying dragon (*Draco volans*) can
also glide through the air, and it has even
more specialized adaptations to help it fly.
This agamid lizard is found in rainforests and
plantations in Malaysia, the Philippines and
Indonesia. On either side of its body, between
the front- and hindlimbs, there is a large flap
of skin supported by extensions of the ribs.

When the lizard is resting or simply climbing
about in the trees, the ribs are drawn into the
side of the lizard's body and the flaps of skin
are folded out of the way. But when the lizard
needs to fly, the ribs are extended, revealing
the flight surfaces. The flying dragon then
launches itself into the air and glides to safety
on its 'wings', staying airborne in this way for
some distance. Like all the other reptiles that
can fly, the flying dragon can only achieve
gliding flight. It has no means of flapping its
'wings' and sustaining itself in the air or
changing direction at will like birds or bats.

Among the skinks (family Scincidae),
species exist that have reduced limbs, like the

Florida sand skink (*Neoseps reynoldsii*) of
the U.S.A. Some skinks have dispensed with
limbs completely and these include the
thin-bodied legless *Acontias* species of Africa
and Madagascar.

The body of a lizard is covered in scales
that vary in shape, texture and colour
depending on the species. Some scales have
smooth surfaces while others are ridged; some
scales butt up to each other and others
overlap; some scales are small and others are
large. In many families, including iguanas
(family Iguanidae), agamids (family
Agamidae) and chameleons (family
Chamaeleonidae), the scales often form spiny
crests and other outgrowths, sometimes
reinforced with bone, that help protect the
lizards from predators. The rare rhinoceros
iguana (*Cyclura cornuta*) of Haiti and some
other islands in the Lesser Antilles gets its
name because of the knobbly outgrowths on
the tip of the male's snout, which resemble a
rhinoceros horn. Jackson's chameleon
(*Chamaeleo jacksonii*) of African savanna
regions goes even further: the male has three
large, prominent horns on his head.

One of the most ornately adorned lizards
is the plumed basilisk (*Basiliscus plumifrons*)
of South America. Not only has it a bony
crest on its head, it also has impressive crests
on its back and tail. The spiny-tailed iguana
(*Ctenosaura pectinata*) is found in forests in
Mexico and Central America. It is about 3-ft
(0.9-m) long, and has a tail equipped with
spiny scales, making it a useful weapon.
When it comes to spikes and spines, however,
the most bizarrely adorned lizard must surely
be the thorny devil or moloch (*Moloch

A common green iguana (Iguana iguana) in typical basking pose.

horridus). Almost every part of the body of this strange-looking denizen of arid Australian scrub and desert is covered in large conical spines. Although the thorny devil is only about 6-in (15-cm) long, not many predators would risk an injury trying to tackle it – which is just as well for the lizard, since it is in reality a harmless creature that feeds on ants. The spines serve another useful function, however: they collect condensed dew that the reptile then drinks. Almost as oddly attired is the Texas horned lizard (*Phrynosoma cornutum*) of the southern U.S.A, which has a short, stocky body flanked by spines; the rear of its head is also fringed with horns. But again, despite its fearsome appearance, it prefers to eat ants and hides away from danger whenever it can.

Far From Tongue-Tied

Anyone who has watched a lizard, perhaps in a zoo or in a home vivarium, will have seen the reptile's tongue flicking in and out as it explores its surroundings. It is in fact picking up minute chemicals, which convey vital information concerning possible food sources, mates, rivals or other dangers. These chemicals are then passed to Jacobson's organ, a group of sensory cells situated in the roof of the mouth near the snout. From there, the vomeronasal nerve transmits the information to the brain. A species such as Gould's monitor (*Varanus gouldii*), that relies heavily on the information it receives from its tongue, flicks it in and out frequently, while other species that have less well-developed sensory apparatus do so less often. Some lizards, such as the green tree gecko

*The gliding lizard (*Holaspis guentheri*), showing expanded ribs and skin flaps that enable it to 'fly'.*

*A male iguana (*Iguana iguana*) in Honduras.*

(*Naultinus elegans*), also use their tongues to wash their eyes, and others poke their tongues out as a form of defence. The most remarkable tongue adaptation is seen in the chameleons, however, as they flick out their long tongues to snatch insects, seemingly out of thin air!

Keeping Safe

The enemies of lizards are legion and include all kinds of birds, from woodpeckers and shrikes to the curious secretary bird of the African bush, snakes, other lizards, mammals such as polecats, badgers, caracals, foxes, and fish. Apart from the protection afforded by their scaly bodies, most lizards can defend themselves by lashing out with their tails or using their sharp teeth and claws. A few lizards are venomous, while others are big enough to avoid the unwanted attentions of hunters, but most species must use other ways to avoid becoming a meal unless they decide to fight. Some of the strategies adopted by lizards for staying alive have already been mentioned. These include tail-shedding (autotomy), gliding to safety, living a life underground, hiding in crevices that are too small for predators to squeeze into, making oneself a thoroughly unpleasant mouthful by virtue of having a body covered in spines, or simply running away as fast as possible when threatened with danger.

The best technique, however, and the one that uses the least energy, is to avoid being seen in the first place. As with many other creatures, this is a useful two-fold strategy. As well as remaining inconspicuous to its enemies, an animal that is hard to see is also

well placed to ambush an unsuspecting meal of its own. Many lizards are nocturnal, hiding under rocks or in tree hollows by day and venturing out under cover of darkness when there are fewer predators about. Lizards that are active by day often use various forms of camouflage to avoid being seen, while tree-dwelling species like iguanas are often coloured green to match their surroundings. The forest iguana (*Polychrus gutterosus*) is marked with dappled shades of green and brown. When it lies on a branch it flattens its body and looks for all the world like part of the foliage. Lizards that live in dry, dusty places are often coloured various shades of brown to help them blend into their habitat, a good example being the wall lizard (*Lacerta muralis*). This is a variably-coloured species, but individuals are usually brownish-red or grey with dark markings – similar colours to the rocks and walls on which they are often found. The masters of disguise in the reptile world are the chameleons; they can even change their colour to match their surroundings (see page 182 et seq.). This feat is also achieved by the chisel-teeth lizards in the family Agamidae.

Sometimes there is nowhere to hide and nowhere to run, and other strategies must be employed when confronted by enemies. The beaded lizards are the only venomous species. Both are vividly marked to advertise the fact that they are poisonous, and when faced with danger they indulge in bouts of hissing and mouth-gaping. Most often this seems to have the desired effect and would-be predators usually retreat. Gaping with a wide-open mouth is also a method employed by the

*The horn-nosed chameleon (*Calumma brevicornis*), photographed in Madagascar. It is using its prehensile tail to grip the branches.*

OPPOSITE
*Marine iguana (*Amblyrhynchus cristatus*). Its sharp claws help it to grip slippery rocks.*

LEFT
*The spiky adornments on the head of the desert horned lizard (*Phrynosoma platyrrhinos*) are used for self-defence.*

Head of a forest lizard, photographed in Tone Sai National Park, Phuket, Thailand.

frilled lizard (*Chlamydosaurus kingii*) of
Australia, but the threat display is augmented
by the erection of a brightly-coloured frill
around the lizard's neck, with the intention of
making it look bigger and fiercer than it really
is. The blue-tongued skink (*Tiliqua
scincoides*) of Australia also opens its mouth
and hisses when cornered, sticking out its
huge, alarming, bright-blue tongue in the
process. The Arabian toad-headed agamid
(*Phrynocephalus mystaceus*) adopts a stiff-
legged defensive posture with tail raised if
alarmed, and then rolls and unrolls its tail.
Movement is often the stimulus for a predator
to attack, so as a last resort some lizards
pretend they are dead in the hope that
predators will lose interest. (Some snakes
adopt the same strategy.) They either become
very rigid, a condition known as tonic
immobility, or they make themselves go limp
and lifeless.

The hooded scaly-foot *Pygopus nigriceps*
of Western Australia is a harmless, snake-
like, limbless lizard. When threatened, it
mimics a poisonous snake known as
Denisonia gouldii. First, the hooded scaly-
foot bends its neck back into an S-shape, just
like a real snake, and rears up in a threat
display, before inflating its throat and hissing.
The armadillo lizard (*Cordylus cataphractus*)
of South Africa has an appropriate name.
About 8.5-in (22-cm) long, the armadillo
lizard's head, back, legs and tail are heavily
protected by spiny scales making it a fairly
slow-moving species, perhaps because of all
this heavy body armour. When confronted by
danger the lizard usually rolls up into a ball,
gripping its tail in its mouth and thus

Ctenosaur lizard (Ctenosaurus
similis), *photographed in Manuel
Antonio National Park, Costa
Rica.*

RIGHT
The Australian frilled lizard
*(*Chlamydosaurus kingii*),*
using its frills to scare and deter
predators.

OPPOSITE
*Sand lizard (*Lacerta agilis*).*

protecting the softer, more vulnerable belly region. Most predators, confronted by this tough, prickly object, decide to look for something else to eat instead.

A few species of lizards are big enough and aggressive enough to make most assailants keep their distance. The family Varanidae contains some very large and powerful species. Gould's monitor (*Varanus gouldii*) of Australia grows to a length of 5ft (1.5m) and roams over large areas of coastal forest and desert seeking out insects, reptiles, birds and mammals to eat. To appear even more intimidating to its enemies, it rears up onto its hindlegs and opens its mouth wide. Another member of this family, the Komodo dragon (*Varanus komodoensis*), is the largest of all living lizards. Heavy-bodied, fierce, with powerful jaws and teeth and strong limbs, the Komodo dragon is capable of devouring prey as large as wild boar and deer

OPPOSITE
*The thorny devil (*Moloch horridus)
is harmless despite its fearsome
appearance.

LEFT
*The Nile monitor (*Varanus niloticus)
is a large, predatory lizard that can
swim.

RIGHT
A green day gecko (Heteropholis
manukanus) *on Stephens Island,
New Zealand.*

OPPOSITE
A male Cook Strait tuatara
(Sphenodon punctatus) *scaling a
tree at night. Stephens Island, New
Zealand.*

and at over 10ft (3m) in length has little to
fear from most other creatures.

Finding Food
The majority of lizards are carnivorous
predators. Depending on the species, their
main food consists of invertebrates such as
insects, spiders and worms, and vertebrates
such as frogs and other amphibians, other
reptiles, birds and mammals. Most prey is
quickly grabbed in the lizard's jaws as soon
as it is in range, then despatched with the aid
of sharp teeth. The chameleons use their
sticky tongues to catch food, while some
lizard species will also raid nests and eat
eggs. The common tegu (*Tupinambis
teguixin*) of Central and northern South
America is a large woodland-dwelling lizard
that often raids villages, eating both chickens
and their eggs.

The arrangement of lizards' jaws means

LIZARDS

that they are not able to open their mouths as wide as snakes, with the result that prey must be smaller than the lizard's mouth if it is to be swallowed whole, otherwise it must first be chewed into pieces. Most burrowing lizards have a narrow head that facilitates movement through the burrows they make in the soil. Ants and termites are often the preferred food of these species, so a small head and small jaws are no impediment to them.

The caiman lizard (*Dracaena guianensis*) of South America is an expert snail-eater. A powerfully built species about 4-ft (1.2-m) long, it inhabits swampy ground and woodland near rivers. The caiman lizard swims and dives well, spending much of its time in the water. When it finds a snail, it takes the prey in its jaws, and tilts its head so

that the snail slides towards the back of the mouth. Here it is broken up by the lizard's crushing, molar-like back teeth, the soft parts of the snail are swallowed and the shell is spat out.

A very small number of lizards are strictly herbivorous, although many species eat vegetation as part of a mixed diet. Sometimes, a reptile's diet changes as it matures, or depending on what food is available. Many iguanas (family Iguanidae) are herbivorous when adult, though they may have eaten insects and other animals when they were juveniles. The common iguana (*Iguana iguana*) of the Americas is a tree-dwelling, herbivorous species, while the chuckwalla (*Sauromalus obesus*) of parts of the southern U.S.A. and Mexico is another plant-eater, often choosing the leaves, flowers and buds of the creosote bush. Other herbivorous lizards include some of

OPPOSITE
*A green lizard (*Lacerta viridis*), showing the effectiveness of its camouflage.*

LEFT
*Gould's monitor (*Varanus gouldii*), photographed in Northern Territory, Australia.*

RIGHT
*Marine iguanas (*Amblyrhynchus
cristatus*) feeding on seaweed-
encrusted rocks within the intertidal
zone on Isla Espanola in the
Galapagos.*

the larger species of Australian skinks
(family Scincidae).

Social Behaviour and Mating
Lizards employ a whole range of social
signals, many of them designed to protect
territorial boundaries or to attract mates. The
majority of lizards are active by day, therefore
most of the signals are highly visual ones.
Lizards can see colour, and the use of colour
is often an important component of their
displays. Some species inflate colourful throat
sacs or other structures when displaying or
confronted by an enemy; others may change
colour completely. For example, the flap-
necked chameleon (*Chamaeleo dilepis*) is

RIGHT
*A lava lizard (*Microlophus
albemarlensis*) feeding on a dead
booby in the Galapagos.*

A Galapagos land iguana (Conolophus subcristatus) *eating opuntia. The cactus provides a source of food and water for these iguanas, which can survive without fresh water for up to a year.*

usually green, yellow or reddish-brown to match the foliage on which it lives. When alarmed, however, it turns green-black and becomes covered in white and yellow spots. Hearing is well-developed in lizards, and hisses and other audible signals are often used to communicate, especially as warnings. Chemical signals are also used in some species; glands are present on the belly, around the thighs and around the cloaca, particularly in males, and their secretions probably attract females and serve as territorial markings.

Many of the territorial warnings issued by lizards involve body movements. These include head movements, bobbing the whole body up and down, inflating the body to make it appear larger, waving the tail and opening the mouth wide. Sometimes displays can go on for hours on end, and although they usually have the desired result in banishing intruders of the same species, they involve the lizard making itself as conspicuous as possible. Such actions, while an essential part of the lizard's repertoire of behaviour, nevertheless expose it to predators such as snakes. One of the fiercest territory defenders is the eastern fence lizard (*Sceloporus undulatus*) of the U.S.A. and Mexico, which vigorously sees off intruding males when it is trying to attract a female for mating.

Sometimes signalling is not sufficient to see off a rival and a fight ensues. At the start of the breeding season, male marine iguanas (*Amblyrhynchus cristatus*) establish territories and fiercely defend them against intruders. These battles go on for some time, but eventually subside as hierarchies become

established. A more spectacular display is seen in Bengal monitors (*Varanus bengalensis*): during the breeding season, males confront each other and prepare to do battle for the right to mate with females. Two opposing males rear up onto their hindlegs, using their powerful tails as props, then grasp

each other around the body with their front legs. Now a titanic wrestling match ensues, each male attempting to push his rival over. Eventually a winner emerges and gains the right to mate.

As in other vertebrates, the courtship rituals of lizards are designed to attract a mate

FAR RIGHT
*Male Namibian rock agamid (*Agama planiceps*).*

*Common iguana (*Iguana iguana*)*
Note the prominent dorsal crest.

and achieve acquiescence so that mating can take place. In some other animal species – for example, some birds – the female solicits the male, but with lizards it is the male that initiates the courtship. For mating to be successful, the female must have mature eggs in her body, and she must signal that she is receptive to the male's overtures. The courtship ritual of the green anole (*Anolis carolinensis*) of the Americas has been studied intensively. Courtship begins with the male engaging in a bout of head-bobbing, coupled with inflation of the dewlap under the throat. He may then approach the female by walking towards her on stiff legs. If the female is ready to mate she will arch her neck and remain still as the male approaches. Sometimes, however, the male's advances are wasted, for the female is not ready to mate and runs away instead. Some lizards use vocal signals to attract a mate; both males and females of the Indian wall gecko (*Hemidactylus flaviviridis*) call in this way.

During courtship, the large Komodo dragon (*Varanus komodoensis*) of parts of South-East Asia approaches the female, using his tongue to pick up scents that tell him if she is ready to mate. Courtship may then continue with the male scratching the female's back with his claws. If she is

*Male lava lizard (*Microlophus delanonis*) perched on a rock and displaying his black throat to attract a female.*

unreceptive to his advances, she hisses and inflates her neck. If she is receptive, however, the male climbs onto her back, rubbing his hindlimbs against the base of her tail and causing her to raise the tail so that mating can occur. The females of a few species of lizards can produce young without a male playing any part in the process (see below). In most species, however, courtship leads to copulation by a male and a female. Males have paired reproductive organs called hemipenes, and internal fertilization takes place within the female's oviducts.

Most lizards produce leathery shelled eggs, although some produce eggs with hard shells. The number of eggs a lizard lays varies according to the species: it may be one or two, up to 40 or more in the case of some chameleons, up to 60 in the Nile monitor (*Varanus niloticus*). The female lizard usually lays her eggs under rocks or logs, in places where the humidity is high. Some species, such as the European chameleon (*Chamaeleo chamaeleon*), lay their eggs in holes in damp soil. The female Tokay gecko (*Gekko gecko*) of Asia lays eggs that have a sticky outer coating, which hardens on contact with the air, gluing the eggs to the surface on which they have been laid. The female common tegu (*Tupinambis teguixin*) of the Americas lays her eggs in the nest of tree-dwelling termites. First she rips open the side of the nest, then she deposits her six or so eggs inside. The termites, always quick to spot any damage to their nest, repair the hole made by the tegu, at the same time sealing the eggs inside. Safe from predators and in a moist, temperature-stable

*Marine iguanas (*Amblyrhynchus cristatus*). These females, on Espanola (Hood) Island, Galapagos, are behaving aggressively towards each other, while another is emerging from her burrow on the right.*

environment, the tegu's eggs incubate safely. Once the young have hatched from their shells they dig themselves out of the termites' nest. The Nile monitor uses a similar strategy, the female laying her eggs in the mounds of termites.

Once they have laid their eggs, most lizards simply leave them to hatch out, but some skinks show a degree of parental care. After the female Great Plains skink (*Eumeces obsoletus*) has laid her 20 or so eggs in a nest beneath a rock, she guards them while they

LIZARDS

RIGHT
*A green anole (*Anolis carolinensis*)*
climbing a branch in the West
Indies.

OPPOSITE LEFT
Eggs of the common or viviparous
*lizard (*Lacerta vivipara*). These thin-*
walled eggs have just been laid by
the female lizard and the young
lizards, visible inside, are about to
hatch.

OPPOSITE RIGHT
A common or viviparous lizard
shortly after birth, hatching out
from its thin-walled egg sac.

incubate, even turning them regularly so that they are evenly warmed. A couple of months later, when the eggs begin to hatch, the mother helps to remove the foetal membranes from the hatchlings. She then cares for the young during the next ten days or so, cleaning them and protecting them from predators.

In some lizards, the eggs are retained within the mother's body and she gives birth to live young. This is known as ovoviviparity. In a few species, such as the spiny-tailed skink (*Egernia stokesii*), the young develop in the female's oviduct and are nourished through a kind of placenta, a condition called viviparity.

As mentioned, there is a condition seen in some groups of animals, including some lizards, called parthenogenesis, or virgin birth. In these species, populations consisting only of females produce viable young from eggs that have not been fertilized by males. The phenomenon is seen in members of various families, including chameleons, agamids, geckos and whiptails. So what is the advantage, if any, of such a method of reproduction? One of the benefits is that only one individual is required to produce the next generation instead of the two individuals that are required when a male and a female of the species mate. Since all members of a parthenogenetic population can produce young, the population can grow more quickly. But there are some downsides, the chief one being that single-sex populations lack the variety in their gene pool that is necessary to adapt quickly to changes in the environment or to combat new diseases. This probably explains why parthenogenesis is not more commonly seen in the animal kingdom.

LIZARD FAMILIES

The suborder Sauria is divided into about 16 families, although the number varies slightly according to different taxonomists. Several families contain members whose future is at risk, mainly due to pressures caused by hunting or habitat destruction, and some species became extinct in the 20th century.

FAMILY AGAMIDAE

The family Agamidae encompasses the chisel-teeth lizards, so-called for the unusual nature of their teeth. Unlike the teeth of most other lizards, theirs are not firmly fixed in sockets. Instead, they are attached to the surfaces of the bones that bear the teeth. The front teeth are frequently chisel-shaped, resembling the incisors of mammals, or they are long and fang-like in shape. The other teeth are either cylindrical with flattish tops or are flattened with shear-like edges. There are

RIGHT
*Anglehead agamid (*Gonocephalus liogaster*) at the Mulu National Park, Sarawak.*

OPPOSITE
Green garden lizard (Calotes, sp.) in its black colour phase. Sinharaja National Park, Sri Lanka.

FAR RIGHT
FAR RIGHT
*The desert agamid (*Agama
mutabilis*) is a diurnal lizard that
lives in rocky and sandy deserts
from North Africa to south-western
Asia.*

about 420 species of agamids split into over
50 genera. As a family, they range from
Africa and Asia to Australia.

Many agamid species are plump-bodied
reptiles with long legs, thin tails and large,
triangular-shaped heads well set off from the
neck. The scales covering the body are
frequently spiny or keeled. Neck frills, throat
fans, crests and other body adornments are
features of many members of this family.
They have well-developed eyes and therefore
good eyesight, and are active by day,
foraging for food on the ground, among rocks
or in the trees. Some species can rapidly
change colour.

Agamids are mainly carnivorous, feeding
on a variety of food items from insects to
eggs, although the Egyptian spiny-tailed
lizard (*Uromastyx aegyptius*) consumes plant
matter. Some members of the family have
developed unusual adaptations for moving
about: the flying dragons (*Draco* species) can
glide from tree to tree using flaps of skin that
extend from the sides of the body (see page
149 et seq.) and steering with the tail; the
Soa-Soa water dragon (*Hydrosaurus
amboinensis*) has a flattened tail to help it
swim; the frilled lizard (*Chlamydosaurus
kingii*) is one of several lizard species that can
run on its hindlegs to escape from danger.
Courtship is an elaborate affair among most
agamids; males vigorously see off rivals and
take part in highly ritualized displays that
often involve parading brightly-coloured
crests and heads. After mating, the female
lays between one and about 27 eggs,
according to the species, while some agamids
give birth to live young.

An agamid in the Sahara desert, North Africa.

RIGHT
*Male ground agamid (*Agama
aculeata*) basking in the sun in the
Kalahari Gemsbok National Park,
South Africa.*

OPPOSITE
*Thorny-tailed agamid (*Agama
stellio*).*

Other well-known members of the family
Agamidae include the common agama (*Agama
agama*) of central African tropical forests, the
curious-looking thorny devil or moloch
(*Moloch horridus*) of the arid parts of
Australia, the eastern water dragon
(*Physignathus leseuerii*) of the coastal region
of eastern Australia and the Arabian toad-
headed agamid (*Phrynocephalus mystaceus*) of
the deserts of south-west Asia.

Conservation status: two species are classed
as Endangered; two species are classed as
Vulnerable.

FAMILY CHAMAELEONIDAE

Depicted in countless stories, used as a logo in
advertising and marketing and imbued with an
almost endearing quality despite their
somewhat bizarre appearance, the chameleons
are possibly the most celebrated of all lizards.
They are best known for their remarkable
ability to change colour at will; in fact, a
person subject to frequent changes of mood or
appearance is often described as 'chameleon-
like'. But being able to change colour is just
one of an array of interesting adaptations
displayed by chameleons, which together help
to make them the most specialized group of
tree-dwelling lizards.

There are about 135 species of
chameleons, and they are to be found in Africa
(except the Sahara), Madagascar (where nearly
half of all chameleon species live) and other
islands of the Indian Ocean, the Indian
subcontinent, parts of the Middle East and
Europe. Although primarily tree-dwelling, a
few species live on the ground. Chameleons

RIGHT
*Namibian rock agamid (*Agama
planiceps*), photographed in
Namibia.*

OPPOSITE
*Agamid lizard (*Agama agama*)
photographed in the Masai Mara,
Kenya.*

RIGHT and OPPOSITE
*This thorny devil (*Moloch horridus*)*
has a cryptic coloration which helps
it to blend in with its surroundings.

feed on a variety of animals such as insects, spiders and scorpions, but the larger species also take birds and small mammals.

The similar lifestyles pursued by the majority of chameleons mean that the basic body shape is also usually similar, although there are considerable detail differences among the various species, and body lengths vary from about 0.75in (2cm) up to about

11in (28cm). Chameleons are typically green, brown or yellow – colours that aid concealment among the branches and foliage of their tree habitats. The head and body are flattened in a leaf-like manner, and there is little or no demarcation between the head and the body. In some species, for example, Jackson's chameleon (*Chamaeleo jacksonii*), there are prominent horns extending from the nose region, while the head of the flap-necked chameleon (*Chamaeleo dilepis*) extends backwards over the neck region, forming a hood. The muscular tail is prehensile: in other words, it can wind around foliage to help the lizard get a more secure grip and remain immobile as it stalks its prey. Chameleons' legs are usually long and slender, and on each foot the toes are arranged in such a way that three grip one side of the branch and two the other to ensure the best hold, meaning that it is zygodactylous. Another remarkable feature of chameleons is their eyes. These protrude on small, turret-like structures on the side of the head, and each eye can be moved up, down or sideways independently of the other. They also give the chameleon a degree of binocular vision, helping it to focus accurately on its prey.

Some other lizards can change their skin colour, but the chameleon is the most accomplished at the task, altering its colour to match the surroundings as it moves about. A chameleon can also change colour if threatened or excited; for example, when confronted by an enemy. In such instances, the chameleon may even introduce other hues and patterns into its repertoire, such as spots and blotches. A complex mechanism lies

OPPOSITE
A female Parson's chameleon (Calumma parsonii). *Her opposable toes help her to grasp branches.*

LEFT
*Oustalet's chameleon (*Furcifer oustaleti) *rummaging among dry banana leaves.*

RIGHT and OPPOSITE
*Panther chameleon (*Furcifer
pardalis*). Note the protective neck
flap typical of many chameleons.*

behind this ability to change colour: the pattern of pigmentation in the skin is under the control of the nervous system, which causes the pigment to expand or contract, thus automatically lightening or darkening the skin in response to the animal's background.

Armed with this impressive array of adaptive features, a chameleon moves slowly and stealthily through the vegetation, looking for food. Even the compressed body gives it an advantage by centring the lizard's weight above the branch onto which it is climbing. Some species even sway in time to the breeze, blending in with the leaves that surround them. Suddenly, one of the chameleon's roving eyes spots a butterfly gently fluttering on a branch above. Now its other eye swivels round so that the butterfly is in sharp focus. Without altering its grip on the branch, the chameleon inches its body forward, lining itself up for the strike. Even though the

RIGHT and OPPOSITE LEFT
Chameleon Furcifer balteatus, *with*
detail of coiled tail.

OPPOSITE RIGHT
Chameleon Furcifer verrucosus.

butterfly is some distance away, the chameleon has another weapon at its disposal. In the blink of an eye, it shoots out a long tongue, securing the butterfly on a sticky pad at its tip. Then the tongue is rapidly withdrawn into the mouth with the prey still attached. The tongue is as long as a chameleon's head and body combined, and is an amazingly effective tool for reaching prey without the need for the reptile to reveal its presence until it is too late for the victim.

Most chameleons have a lively courtship display, often involving fights between rival males. Male and female European chameleons (*Chamaeleo chamaeleon*) sometimes bite each other while mating. After mating, the sperm is stored in the female's body for some time and eggs are usually laid in holes in the ground. Depending on the species, between four and 40 eggs are usually laid, although it could be more in some species. A few species give birth to live young, including Jackson's chameleon (*Chamaeleo jacksonii*) and

LIZARDS

Meller's chameleon (*Chamaeleo mellerii*).

The stump-tailed chameleon known as *Brookesia spectrum* is a small species, brown in colour and bearing a close resemblance to the leaves that litter the forest floor where it lives in parts of East Africa. Its tail is not prehensile like those of other chameleons, but is short and stumpy. It also has tiny outgrowths on its head and body that mimic the appearance of a decaying leaf as it creeps about on the ground looking for insects to eat. Its appearance and extremely slow movements not only help it to approach its prey without been seen, but also help it to avoid the unwanted attentions of predators.

Conservation status: one species is classed as Critically Endangered; one species is Endangered; four other species are Vulnerable.

FAMILY IGUANIDAE

About 690 species make up the family Iguanidae, most of which are confined to the New World, being found principally from southern Canada to Argentina, although a few species live in Madagascar, Tonga and Fiji. The family has exploited a wide variety of habitats, including forests, grassland, scrub and desert, coasts and even the sea. The iguanids can be considered as the New World equivalents of the Old World agamids (family Agamidae), and for this reason their distributions do not overlap. Species such as the common or green iguana (*Iguana iguana*)

ABOVE
A chameleon discovered in open woodland near Zomba, Malawi.

RIGHT
Chameleon Brookesia peyrierasi *on the rainforest floor in Madagascar.*

OPPOSITE
Chameleon Furcifer lateralis.

LIZARDS

BELOW RIGHT
*Iguana (*Iguana iguana*), showing characteristic banded coloration on the body and tail that aids camouflage in trees and on the forest floor.*

OPPOSITE
*Basilisk or Jesus Christ lizard (*Basiliscus basiliscus*), so-called because of its ability to 'walk' on water.*

of the Americas and the plumed basilisk (*Basiliscus plumifrons*) of South America are among the species most often kept in zoos or as pets; therefore some members of the family are quite familiar. As might be expected from such a large and ubiquitous group of reptiles, iguanids vary widely in terms of their size, appearance and habits. All iguanids are active by day, many feed on insects or bigger animal prey, but some are omnivorous or vegetarian. The common iguana, which can reach a length of 6.5ft (2m), is strictly vegetarian, as are the chuckwallas (*Sauromalus obesus*) of the U.S.A. and Mexico and the marine iguana (*Amblyrhynchus cristatus*) of the Galapagos Islands. Some species are mainly terrestrial but often take to the water and swim.

RIGHT
*A black chuckwalla (*Sauromalus
hispidus) *in Arizona.*

OPPOSITE
*The chuckwalla (*Sauromalus
obesus)*, a large lizard that lives in
south-western deserts in the U.S.A.
and Mexico.*

*The piebald chuckwalla (*Sauromalus varius*) is a visually-orientated lizard that communicates using colour and behaviour displays.*

LEFT
*This chuckwalla (*Sauromalus obesus*) is a diurnal lizard, basking in the early morning sun until it reaches its optimum body temperature, when it forages for food.*

RIGHT and OPPOSITE LEFT
Marine iguanas (Amblyrhynchus
cristatus).

OPPOSITE RIGHT
Land iguanas (Conolophus
subcristatus) *live in arid parts of the
Galapagos archipelago and feed on
the opuntia cactus.*

RIGHT and OPPOSITE
*Galapagos land iguana (*Conolophus
subcristatus*).*

*Spiny lizard (*Sceloporus undulatus*).*

At mating time, and when defending territories, many iguana species indulge in ritualized displays that may involve head-bobbing, inflating throat sacs, hissing and using other highly visual or audible signals. The territorial defence of marine iguanas involves males engaging in bouts of head-butting in an attempt to push one another over. The spiny-tailed iguana (*Ctenosaura pectinata*) of Mexico and Central America is gregarious as well as territorial, living together in colonies with a dominant male as the head of the group. Most iguanids lay eggs, the number per clutch varying from one to about 40, depending on the species. However, some species give birth to live young.

Other common species of iguana include the green anole (*Anolis carolinensis*) of the Americas, the well-armoured Texas horned lizard (*Phrynosoma cornutum*) of arid parts of the southern U.S.A., the impressively-marked collared lizard (*Crotaphytus collaris*) of the southern U.S.A. and Mexico and the Madagascan iguanas (*Oplurus* species), characterized by the rings of spiny scales on their tapering tails.

Conservation status: five species are Critically Endangered; two species are Endangered; seven species ar Vulnerable.

FAMILY GEKKONIDAE

This is one of the largest families of lizards, with about 1,073 species of geckos recognized worldwide, occurring in tropical, subtropical and warm zones of the world from about 50° N to about 47° S. They are

A distinctive collared lizard (Crotaphytus collaris) on a fossilized tree trunk in a petrified forest in Arizona.

OPPOSITE
*A keeled earless lizard (*Holbrookia propinqua*) rests in shadows on the National Seashore Reserve, Padre Island, Texas.*

LEFT
*Lesser earless lizard (*Holbrookia maculata*), Saguaro National Monument, Arizona. The loss of its ear is thought to be an adaptation to the lizard's habit of burrowing head-first into the sand.*

OPPOSITE
*Desert horned lizard (*Phrynosoma platyrrhinos*).*

LEFT
Desert iguana (Dipsaurus dorsalis), showing nostril, eye and external ear or tympanum.

LIZARDS

BELOW RIGHT
Day gecko (genus Phelsuma).

FAR RIGHT
Cryptic diurnal gecko (Lygodactylus tuberosus).

OPPOSITE LEFT
*A New Zealand forest gecko (*Hoplodactylus granulatus*) camouflaged on a tree trunk.*

OPPOSITE RIGHT
Gecko Tarentola annularis.

particularly common in the tropics. The habitats that geckos occupy are varied, ranging from forests, wetlands, mountains and deserts wherever the temperature does not drop too low and wherever there is sufficient insect and other small invertebrate food supplies for them to eat. Geckos are usually seen in hues of brown, black or grey, although some are yellow, green or orange, with small scales embedded in a softer skin than many other lizards. Typically, a gecko has a slightly flattened, broadly triangular-shaped head and a stout neck. The body and tail are also slightly depressed, the flattened shape helping them to remain concealed on branches and other backgrounds. Geckos range in size from about 0.6in (16mm) in the case of the dwarf gecko (*Sphaerodactylus ariasae*) – believed to be the world's smallest reptile – to about 11in (28cm) or more in the case of the Tokay gecko (*Gekko gecko*). The name 'gecko' probably arose from the sound of the calls made by these lizards.

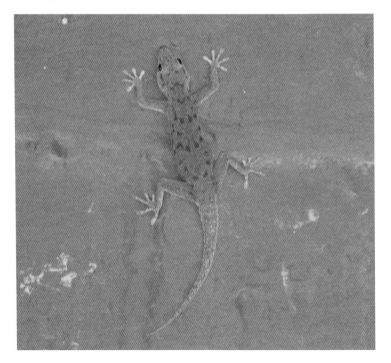

OPPOSITE
*Green day gecko (*Heteropholis
manukanus*), Stephens Island, New
Zealand.*

FAR LEFT
Gecko Hemidactylus brookii
angulatos.

LEFT
*Green tree gecko (*Naultinus
elegans*). Many geckos are relatively
soft-skinned compared with other
reptiles.*

Body and tail shapes vary greatly
according to the species. In some, notably the
white-spotted gecko (*Tarentola annularis*) of
Africa, the body is short and stout, bulging
slightly in the middle, and the tail is short and
tapering. Kuhl's gecko (*Ptychozoon kuhlii*) of
South-East Asia has a curious scaly tail. The
green day gecko (*Heteropholis manukanus*) of
New Zealand has a slim body with a long,
slender tail. Limbs are also variable in
geckos; in some they are long, in others they
are short and stout. Most species have
specially-adapted feet bearing ridges and tiny,
hair-like scales on the underside, designed to

help them grip surfaces securely. The Tokay gecko (*Gekko gecko*) has up to 150,000 such scales on each foot which also branch into tiny end-plates to increase the surface area even more, and which can be pushed into the tiniest of irregularities on a surface. Using their special feet, geckos can climb smooth, vertical surfaces with ease and can even walk upside-down on house ceilings. Some geckos have a similar arrangement of tiny scales on the undersides of their tails, and these are thought to further assist with gripping the surface on which they are climbing.

The eyes of geckos are usually large in comparison with the size of their heads, as befits a group of reptiles that are for the most part nocturnal. Most species have permanently closed, transparent eyelids; sometimes the short, broad tongue is flicked out to wipe the eyelids clean.

Most geckos rely on their cryptic coloration, flattened bodies and nocturnal habits to avoid detection by predators, but some have devised methods of combating enemies should they be spotted. Shedding the tail before escaping is a strategy adopted by many, and flying geckos can leap from a tree and glide to safety. Williams' diplodactyl (*Diplodactylus williamsii*) of Australia has the ability to squirt a sticky liquid from glands at the top of its tail; should it be pursued by a predator, for example a wolf spider, the strands entangle it and save the gecko from capture.

Geckos lay few eggs, one to three being the usual number. The eggs are normally hard-shelled and calcareous, and in some species have a sticky outer coating that helps

them to adhere to surfaces. A few geckos lay leathery shells, and a small number give birth to live young.

The large Tokay gecko of Asia and Indonesia is often considered to bring good luck by its presence in the house. Perhaps it has earned this reputation from its habit of eating cockroaches, mice and smaller lizards that aren't such welcome house guests! One of the most striking of all geckos is *Phelsuma vinsonii* of the Mauritius Islands. This species is active by day, and males bear bright-red spots on a green and blue back; females have similar but duller patterning. Although insects form the mainstay of its diet, it also eats nectar and fruit such as bananas.

OPPOSITE
A cryptic leaf gecko mimics a dead leaf.

LEFT and BELOW
*Leaf-tailed gecko (*Uroplatus fimbriatus*) in a threatening posture. Note that pupils are reduced to narrow slits by day.*

OPPOSITE and LEFT
A leaf-tailed gecko in Madagascar.

LIZARDS

*A day gecko (*Phelsuma quadriocellata*).*

In some systems of classification the Gekkonidae is further split into two more families. One of these, the family Diplodactylidae or south-west Pacific geckos, contains geckos that live in New Zealand, New Caledonia and Australia (except southern Victoria and Tasmania). The second, the family Eublepharidae or eyelid geckos, includes species that inhabit parts of North and South America, East and West Africa, India, Asia, Borneo, Malaysia, the Ryukyu Islands, Vietnam and China.

Conservation status: one species is classed as Critically Endangered; three species are Endangered; eight species are Vulnerable.

FAMILY PYGOPODIDAE

The snake-lizards are a family of limbless reptiles. Although they superficially resemble true snakes, they are different anatomically and are in fact most closely related to the geckos (family Gekkonidae), sharing with them features such as fused eyelids and the ability to make sounds. Like geckos, snake-lizards also have fleshy forked tongues that are often extended well out of the mouth. Colours range from brown to grey or black. There are about 36 or so species of snake-lizards (which are also sometimes called scaly-foot lizards), and they range across Australia and New Guinea.

The long, slender body of a snake-lizard enables it to burrow underground, and many species spend much time in the soil. Most species are nocturnal, and all are carnivorous, feeding on a range of creatures from insects to small lizards like geckos.

LIZARDS

Snake-lizards lay one or two elongated eggs. The most widespread member of the family is Burton's snake-lizard (*Lialis burtonis*), a species that can adapt to habitats ranging from semidesert to rainforest. It grow to about 2ft (0.6m) in length and is active both day and night. Using its long, backward-pointing teeth, it quickly overpowers prey.

Conservation status: six species are classed as Vulnerable.

FAMILY TEIIDAE
The Teiidae, also known as the whiptails, are found in the Americas and the West Indies. There are about 280 species in the family, some of which grow to about 4.5ft (1.4m) in length. Active by day, teiids inhabit wetlands, tropical rainforests, savanna and desert, where they feed on a wide variety of prey, including insects, molluscs, fish, frogs, lizards, birds and mammals, while many species hunt for their food in trees, caves, on the ground and in the water. Teiids are slender lizards with large heads, stout bodies and long, whip-like tails. The large and powerful caiman lizard (*Dracaena guianensis*), growing to a length of 4ft (1.2m), is a strong swimmer with a long, flattened tail that it uses like an oar to propel itself through the water.

In the breeding season, many male teiids sport bright breeding colours. The strand racerunner (*Cnemidophorus lemniscatus*) is a fast-running lizard that is adorned with blue patterns on its throat and feet and yellow coloured spots and red stripes along the back and sides. When mating, the male grabs hold of the female's neck in his mouth.

The common tegu (*Tupinambis teguixin*) is a large, robust species that lives in forests in Central and northern South America. It is often trapped by local people who use it as a source of meat, the fat often being used as a cure for ailments.

Conservation status: one species is Critically Endangered; one species is Vulnerable.

FAMILY LACERTIDAE
The 225 or so species of wall and sand lizards are conspicuous, active reptiles found in Europe, Africa and Asia. The viviparous lizard (*Lacerta vivipara*) is found within the Arctic Circle, although no other species of lizard can tolerate such cool conditions. Lacertids are primarily ground-living lizards and are often found in dry, sandy places, including rocky outcrops, while a few are found in grassland and among tropical vegetation. Most species eat insects and

*Melanistic viviparous lizards (*Lacerta vivipara).

suggests, the viviparous lizard is a species that gives birth to live young, usually about five to eight at a time, but the majority lay eggs in holes in the ground.

Conservation status: one species is classed as Critically Endangered; one species is classed as Endangered; six species are classed as Vulnerable.

FAMILY XANTUSIIDAE
The Xantusiidae are known as night lizards, since they begin their hunting activities at dusk but spend the day hiding under rocks, logs or clumps of low-growing vegetation. There are about 21 species in the family which is found in the south-west U.S.A., Mexico, Central America and Cuba. They often inhabit rocky places, where most species feed on nocturnal insects. The desert night lizard (*Xantusia vigilis*) frequents yucca plants and agaves and feeds on termites and flies. Unusually, the island night lizard (*Xantusia riversiana*) is active by day and feeds on flowers and seeds.

With their immobile eyelids and broadly triangular heads, night lizards superficially resemble geckos (family Gekkonidae), but unlike geckos they have prominent scales on their bodies. Night lizards give birth to live young; usually, as is the case with the desert night lizard, between one and three offspring are born at a time. However the island night lizard gives birth to up to nine young.

Conservation status: one species is classed as Vulnerable.

OPPOSITE
*Wall lizard (*Lacerta muralis*).*

LEFT
*A shovel-snouted lizard (*Meroles anchietae*) on a sand dune in Namibia.*

other invertebrates, but a few eat other lizards, snakes and small mammals. Fruit and seeds also figure in the diet of some species.

Most lacertids are small to medium-sized, slender-bodied lizards with long, whip-like tails. One of the largest species is the green lizard (*Lacerta viridis*), that can reach a length of 18in (46cm); in fact, the green lizard is the largest to be found north of the European Alps. Among lacertids, body coloration is variable according to where the species lives: thus *Lacerta muralis* is frequently brownish-red or grey to make it inconspicuous on walls. The lacertids are often agile climbers, and those living among rocks have compressed bodies to enable them to squeeze into small crevices in search of

food or to escape the attentions of predators. Species that live in deserts usually have specially-adapted feet to help them to run over sand. Thus the fringe-toed lizard (*Acanthodactylus boskianus*) has toes bordered with comb-like scales to increase the surface area of its feet and prevent it from sinking into the sand.

Males can be distinguished from females by their larger heads and their more conspicuous colours. Lacertids are territorial, and postures and threat displays are common, particularly during the breeding season when males display with the head tilted upward and the throat expanded, while the females of many lacertids wave their front legs as a signal that they are ready to mate. As its name

*A Namaqua sand lizard (*Pedioplanis namaquensis*) at the entrance of a burrow in the Kalahari Gemsbok National Park, South Africa.*

*A green lizard (*Lacerta viridis*) seen in the Dordogne, France.*

RIGHT
*Spotted sand lizard (*Pedioplanis
lineocellata*).*

OPPOSITE
*Sand lizard (*Lacerta agilis*).*

OPPOSITE
Shingle-back (bobtail) skink
(Trachydosaurus rugosus) *basking in*
the sun.

LEFT
*Black skink (*Mabuya striata sparsa*),*
seen in the Kalahari Gemsbok
National Park, South Africa.

FAMILY SCINCIDAE

The skink family comprises 1,400 species, making it the largest of all lizard families. Skinks occur on every continent except Antarctica, but they are at their most abundant in South-East Asia and Australasia. Skinks are an extremely varied family in terms of both the habitats they occupy and their appearances and lifestyles. They may be found in all kinds of locations, from forests to deserts, where they burrow below the ground, live on the ground or dwell in trees. They eat a variety of food items, ranging from insects to larger animals. Some are herbivorous, however, particularly the larger species, and some are omnivorous.

Skinks often have aquatic habitats, and many can swim well. The marine skink

OPPOSITE
A Himalayan skink at 12,000ft
(3660m) in Kashmir. Note the mites
at the base of the foreleg.

LEFT
Algerian or berber skinks
(Novoeumenes algeriensis) *occur in*
Morocco and Algeria. Males fight
vigorously during the breeding
season.

(*Emoia atrocostata*) lives near coasts where it feeds on crabs and other crustaceans that it finds in the intertidal zone, diving under water to escape from predators. Many ground-dwelling skinks hide under logs or rocks when not searching for food. The tree-dwelling green-blood skink (*Prasinohaema virens*) is well camouflaged in its arboreal habitat. Not only are the back and sides of the reptile's body green but so are its tongue and mouth lining – even its eggs are green.

To describe a typical skink is almost impossible, although most possess certain features such as scales that form a symmetrical shield on the head, and tiny limbs. In many species there is very little differentiation between the small head and the often elongated and somewhat depressed body. The elongated body and tiny limbs reach their extreme development in species such as the Florida sand skink (*Neoseps reynoldsii*) of the U.S.A., in which species the limbs are too small to be of any use for walking. Instead of crawling or using what limbs it has, the Florida sand skink burrows into sand, undulating its body in a kind of swimming action as it moves along and feeding on termites and beetle larvae. Other skinks with greatly reduced limbs include the round-bodied skink (*Chalcides bedriagai*) of

LIZARDS

Europe and Sundeval's skink (*Riopa sundevallii*) of the African plains. Sundeval's skink usually lives underground but comes to the surface in search of insects and other invertebrates to eat, when it proceeds along the ground with a snake-like movement.

The thin-bodied legless skinks (*Acontias* species) of Africa and Madagascar have lost their limbs altogether and have been left with cylindrical bodies and short tails. Because they burrow underground, their eyes and ears are protected by scales, and the lower eyelids have transparent coverings that enable them to see as they dig through the soil. *Feylinia cussori* of tropical Africa is a large, legless skink about 14in (36cm) in length, in which species the demarcation between head and body is even harder to discern. A local legend has it that the skink can enter a person's body at will, the unfortunate host dying when it leaves.

However, there are many, such as the brown skink (*Scincella lateralis*) of the U.S.A., that are 'typically' lizard-like, with slender bodies, tapering tails and well-proportioned limbs. The Australian western blue-tongued skink (*Tiliqua occipitalis*) has a stout body with a large head and a small tapering tail, its bluish body marked with brown bands. This is a big skink – about 18-in (46-cm) long that sometimes shelters in rabbit burrows. When alarmed, it opens its mouth to reveal a big, fleshy blue tongue. Another plump-bodied, short-tailed species is the spiny-tailed skink (*Egernia stokesii*), in which the body and tail are covered in sharp spines that help to protect it.

The reproductive habits of skinks vary:

some, like Sundeval's skink, lay eggs, and some, such as the spiny-tailed skink, give birth to live young.

Conservation status: two species are classed as Critically Endangered; three are classed as Endangered; 20 species are classed as Vulnerable.

FAMILY CORDYLIDAE

The girdled and plated lizards, of which there are about 84 species, are found in Africa and Madagascar, and most frequent rocky or arid

environments south of the Sahara Desert where they are active during the day. There is much variety of body form within the family, related to the different niches that individual species occupy, the body of a typical cordylid being covered with bony plates underlying the scales. Most members of the family feed on insects or larger prey, but a few are vegetarians.

Those that dwell within rocky crevices, such as the imperial flat lizard (*Platysaurus imperator*), have a head, body, tail and limbs that are flattened laterally to make it easier to

FAR RIGHT
*The Pungwe flat lizard (*Platysaurus pungweensis pungweensi*) is native to the Eastern Highlands of Zimbabwe and neighbouring Mozambique.*

squeeze into tight places where predators cannot enter. The South African armadillo lizard (*Cordylus cataphractus*) can also squeeze into small spaces, but it can also roll up into a ball when danger threatens. Its body is covered with sharp spines which, when rolled up, is an unpalatable prospect for most predators. Some cordylids are thin, elongate reptiles with reduced limbs and very long tails, such a species being the Transvaal snake lizard (*Chamaesaura aena*) of South Africa, which moves quickly through the grass with the help of undulating, snake-like movements of its body.

Many species in the family lay eggs, but a few bear up to six live young. The flat lizards lay elongated, flattened eggs that fit into the

FAR LEFT
*The forelimbs of the large-scaled grass lizard (*Chamaesaura macrolepis*) are absent and the hindlimbs are vestigial spikes.*

LEFT
*Cape girdled lizard (*Cordylus niger*) photographed on Table Mountain, Cape Town, South Africa.*

narrow crevices in which they hide. Some systems of classification separate certain members of the family Cordylidae off into a separate family, the family Gerrhosauridae, whose members are found in most parts of Africa south of the Sahara and in Madagascar.

Conservation status: five species are classed as Vulnerable.

FAMILY DIBAMIDAE

The 15 species of burrowing or blind lizards live in parts of South-East Asia and New Guinea. They are all adapted to a life spent burrowing among rotting logs or in soil, and are consequently legless, worm-like creatures whose eyes are hidden beneath the skin. They are about 6-in (15-cm) long. Much of their biology is unknown, but they are believed to be insectivorous and to lay calcareous eggs. Species include the Mexican blind lizard (*Anelytropsis papillosus*) and the Asian blind lizards of the genus Dibamus.

Conservation status: five species are classed as Vulnerable.

FAMILY XENOSAURIDAE

There are six species of xenosaurs, or crocodile lizards, five of which live in Central America and Mexico (*Xenosaurus* species) and one in China (*Shinisaurus crocodilurus*). Xenosaurs have stout bodies, well-developed heads and tails that are moderately long. The eyes are fairly large, and the mouth bears a forked tongue and fang-like teeth. The biggest species is about 6-in (15-cm) long. Xenosaurs are terrestrial species, usually inhabiting

OPPOSITE
*Cape crag lizard (*Pseudocordylus microlepidotus*), photographed on Table Mountain, Cape Town, South Africa.*

FAR LEFT
*A Karoo girdled lizard (*Cordylus polyzonus*) eating a beetle, Namaqualand, South Africa.*

narrow crevices or living hidden among tree roots; but occasionally they climb trees or enter the water. They lead secretive lives and are most active at dusk. Food includes fish, tadpoles and insects. When threatened, they open their mouths wide, and they have a fierce bite. All species give birth to live young.

FAMILY ANGUIDAE

The 110 or so species of anguids are elongated, snake-like lizards found in many parts of the Old World as well as the New, occupying a range of habitats from hot, arid environments to cool forests. Colours range from green, brown, grey, silver and black, and the largest species grow to about 12in (30cm) in length. The body is covered in bony plates that give the lizards a rigid appearance. However, there are softer scales located along the sides of the body that allow expansion and movement when feeding, breathing or producing eggs. The eyes of most species are small with movable eyelids, and the ear openings are external. Many species have tiny limbs or, in the case of species like the slow-worm (*Anguis fragilis*) of Europe, Asia and Africa and the glass snake (*Ophisaurus apodus*) of Europe and Asia, no limbs at all. Notably different, however, are the alligator lizards of North and Central America, whose body shape is more like that of a 'typical' lizard, with a well-defined head and legs and a slim body and long tail. The southern alligator lizard (*Gerrhonotus multicarinatus*) of the U.S.A. is an adept climber and uses its tail to hang from bushes when raiding eggs from birds's nests.

Many anguids are terrestrial, living under stones and logs, among grass, or burrowing in the soil. A wide variety of food is eaten across the group, with many species feeding on invertebrates such as insects, worms, spiders, grasshoppers and larvae. Larger prey is also taken, including slugs, snails, other lizards, rodents such as mice, and the eggs and young of birds. The majority of anguids lay eggs, ranging in number from two to 12 in each clutch, but some, like the California legless lizard (*Anniella pulchra*), bear live young. Prior to mating, the males of many species engage in aggressive and competitive displays.

Conservation status: three species are classed as Critically Endangered; one species is classed as Endangered; one species is classed as Vulnerable.

FAMILY HELODERMATIDAE

The family Helodermatidae encompasses the beaded lizards and consists of just two members, the Gila monster (*Heloderma suspectum*) and the Mexican beaded lizard (*Heloderma horridum*). Both of these are to be found in dry habitats in the Colorado river region of the U.S.A. and along the Pacific coast of Mexico. A feature unique to these

OPPOSITE
*Head of an alligator lizard (*Elgaria coerulea*), Marin County, California.*

ABOVE
*Slow-worm (*Anguis fragilis*).*
The female is light and the male is a darker colour.

Adult and young slow-worms (Anguis fragilis), *sharing a compost heap with a toad.*

lizards is that they are poisonous. Venom is produced in modified salivary glands in the lower jaw, and when the lizards bite their prey the venom is transferred in the bite from the grooved teeth, when it affects the nervous system. A bite from a beaded lizard is a painful experience for a human being, but it is rarely fatal unless the victim is in poor health.

Both the Gila monster and the beaded lizard are heavy-bodied, stumpy-tailed creatures with boldly-patterned skin. The tails of both species are used to store fat for times when food is scarce. The Gila monster reaches a length of about 2ft (0.6m), and the Mexican beaded lizard grows to about 3ft (0.9m). Beaded lizards live on the ground and shelter by day under rocks or in a burrow, particularly one that has been abandoned by a mammal. At dusk or during the night they emerge to hunt their prey, which consists of mammals, birds and their eggs and amphibians such as frogs. Beaded lizards are generally slow-moving, but can react quickly if provoked. Between three and 13 eggs are produced in late summer, the female burying them in soil and leaving them to incubate.

Conservation status: both species of beaded lizards are classed as Vulnerable.

FAMILY LANTHANOTIDAE
There is just one species in this family, the Bornean earless lizard (*Lanthanotus borneensis*). A drab brown or black reptile about 8-in (20-cm) long, it gets its name because of its lack of external ear openings. It has a rather flattened body and short, powerful limbs, each ending in five claws.

The eyes are tiny, with movable eyelids, the lower eyelid having a transparent 'window'.

Little is known of the habits of this lizard in the wild, although it has been observed in captivity. It seems to be partly aquatic because it takes to water readily, using its forelimbs to help it to swim, and it is also a capable burrower. It moves with sideways undulations on water and on land, where its movements are rather laboured and awkward. Captive specimens eat marine fish, egg yolks and worms. The Bornean earless lizard is active at night and lays eggs.

FAMILY VARANIDAE
The 55 members of the family Varanidae are known as monitor lizards and are found from Africa, through the Middle East to southern Asia, Indonesia and Australia. They occupy habitats ranging from deserts and grasslands to forests and coastal margins. Monitors possess muscular bodies and tails, distinctive necks and narrow, pointed heads. The tongue is forked, like a snake's, and the teeth are sharp and fang-like. The strong limbs terminate in feet equipped with five strong claws. All monitors are voracious meat-eaters,

*Monitor lizard (*Varanus salvator*).*

consuming their prey whole whenever they can. In some places where large, natural mammalian carnivores are absent, such as Australia, monitors have evolved to assume the role of top land predators. They are active by day, many searching out food using their tongues to detect the scent of prey, but others lie in ambush. Prey include insects, snails, carrion, other reptiles' eggs and young, fish, birds and mammals, from shrews to large grazers such as deer.

The monitors include the biggest of all lizards – the Komodo dragon (*Varanus komodoensis*) of the Indonesian islands, where 10-ft (3-m) long specimens are not

OPPOSITE
*A rock monitor (*Varanus exanthematicus) *basking.*

LEFT and BELOW
*A monitor lizard (*Varanus salvator),
seen by the Kinabatangan river estuary, Malaysia.

*Merten's water monitor (*Varanus mertensii*), Northern Territory, Australia.*

uncommon. Prey the size of pigs and deer frequently form part of their diet, and there are instances of Komodo dragons overpowering animals as large as water buffalo weighing 1,300lb (590kg) or more. A large Komodo can easily consume a pig in one meal, and to further add to its sinister reputation it has been known to eat human beings. Even if a victim is not actually eaten, a bite from a Komodo dragon can lead to serious consequences because of the extremely harmful bacteria it carries in its mouth. Some other monitors are also impressively large, even if they do not reach the length achieved by the Komodo dragon. For example, the Nile monitor (*Varanus niloticus*) of Africa grows to about 6.5ft (2m) in length.

Monitors are mostly terrestrial, but a few take readily to water and are powerful swimmers. The common Asiatic monitor (*Varanus salvator*) has been spotted swimming far out at sea and can dive under water for an hour or so if needed. The Nile monitor climbs trees and also swims and dives well. Gould's monitor (*Varanus gouldii*) of Australia can move extremely fast – outrunning even a human being over short distances.

Monitors are highly territorial and use strategies such as rearing up onto their hindlegs, lashing their tails, hissing loudly and holding their heads erect in an attempt to intimidate rivals or enemies. Fighting between rival males at breeding time is common, with individuals sometimes engaging in wrestling bouts to determine which will mate with the females. Depending on the species, up to about 35 eggs are laid following mating.

These are usually placed in holes in banks or trees by water courses.

Conservation status: two species are classed as Vulnerable, including the Komodo dragon.

WORM-LIZARDS

Perhaps the most curious of all the reptiles is the group known as the worm-lizards, ringed lizards or amphisbaenids. The first fossils of worm-lizards appear in rocks dating back to the Paleocene period of North America some 65 million years ago and ancient fossils have also been found in places as far apart as England, Belgium and Tanzania. They are not true lizards, despite their name, but form a

*Desert monitor (*Varanus griseus*) in the Sahara Desert, North Africa.*

distinct suborder (the Amphisbaenia) within the order Squamata, which also contains the lizards and the snakes. Today there are about 140 living species of worm-lizards split into four (sometimes three) families. They vary in size from about 4–30in (10–76cm), but most species fall within the range of 6–15in (15–38cm). Most worm-lizards are found in the subtropical regions of South America and Africa, but some also live in the warmer parts of North America, the West Indies, the Iberian Peninsula, parts of the Middle East and western Asia. Worm-lizards are not especially long-lived, those in captivity normally having a lifespan of about two years.

It is hardly surprising that the worm-lizards occupy their own separate suborder, for they have an array of features that set them apart from all other reptiles. At first glance, a typical worm-lizard could easily be mistaken for a small snake, or even a large worm, for in members of three of the four families the cylindrical, elongated body lacks all trace of external limbs, and they may even have lost all vestiges of the original internal skeletal pelvic and pectoral girdles that once supported the limbs of their ancestors. The only family of worm-lizards that has limbs are the Bipedidae, or Mexican worm-lizards, which have two tiny front legs, each with five clawed toes. Although the limbs are small, they are very powerful, while the body is extremely elongated. In all worm-lizards the body scales form a series of concentric rings along the body, enhancing the segmented, worm-like appearance but also giving rise to their alternative name of ringed lizards. In some species the tail is pointed, but in others it

OPPOSITE
*Nile monitor (*Varanus niloticus*),*
showing forked tongue.

LEFT
The blindworm or worm-lizard
*(*Blanus cinereus*) is a blind and*
legless lizard which burrows into the
ground in arid locations.

is rounded and bears horny scales. Worm-lizards have no external ear-openings and their eyes are tiny and covered by scales. In terms of colour, worm-lizards range from whitish through red-brown and purplish-pink to black. Some species have mottling, spots and other markings.

All worm-lizards are carnivorous, their prey including small, soil-dwelling invertebrates like worms and insects such as ants and termites; some of the larger species also include small vertebrate animals in their diet. Prey can be heard, or even smelt, crawling about in the ground, causing the worm-lizard to immediately home in on its victim; its ears are specially adapted so that the eardrum lies in a forward position at the side of the jaw, and is therefore closer to the source of the sound.

The powerful head of a worm-lizard contains equally strong teeth and jaws and prey is soon torn apart and swallowed. Because water is not freely available beneath the soil, some moisture is obtained from their food, although some species can also 'suck' water from the soil through capillary action. A worm-lizard's mainly subterranean life is one of relative safety, avoiding many of the predators that stalk the ground above. However, various species of snake also live a burrowing life, and several of these are partial to worm-lizards.

Digging in the Dark

The second unusual feature of worm-lizards, and the one that largely explains the curious body adaptations described above, is their lifestyle. All worm-lizards live an exclusively subterranean existence, and although many other reptiles live underground for part of the time, worm-lizards are the only ones to spend their whole lives in this way, apart from rare forays to the surface in search of better places to burrow. The loss of external limbs, the long, thin body, the lack of external ear-openings and the tiny eyes are all adaptations to a life spent burrowing in the dark. Worm-lizards prefer to live in moist soil, where they can build tunnel systems that will remain in place after they have burrowed through. They often build their tunnels close to termite nests, a popular source of food.

Worm-lizards use powerful thrusting and digging movements of the head when making burrows, and they have even more special adaptations to help them in this task. The skulls are more strongly built than in other reptile species, and in some cases they are further strengthened by the addition of keratin (the material that forms hair, feathers and horn in other animals) or by special, low-friction scales that help them to move through the soil. The nostrils face backward and close when the worm-lizard is digging, thus preventing soil from clogging them up. The upper lip closes over the lower lip when the mouth is closed, which also helps prevent soil from entering when the animal is burrowing. A variety of different tunnelling strategies are used by worm-lizards according to the species: the principal digging action involves bracing itself against the tunnel wall by drawing up the loosely attached skin of the body like a set of bellows to effect a secure hold, then battering the soil in front with the head to force its way through. In some species, after the head has thrust into the soil and made some forward progress, it is then pushed up into the tunnel roof to widen it. Other species have refined the tunnel-widening process by using a separate set of special muscles to press the loose soil against the walls of the tunne after the head has been used to make the initial thrust.

Worm-lizards can move backward in their tunnels as well as forward, and this ability, coupled with the fact that some species have swollen tail regions resembling their front ends, has led to myths that the reptiles have two heads. For example, in ancient Roman literature, the amphisbaenid is referred to as a two-headed monster. This physical peculiarity is often used to good advantage. The white-bellied worm-lizard or two-headed blind snake (*Amphisbaena alba*) of tropical South African and Trinidadian rainforests is often found crawling over the forest floor in its search for food. If confronted by danger, it will wave its tail in the air as though it were its head. This usually causes an enemy to attack the tail, leaving the more vulnerable head intact. Once a worm-lizard sheds its tail in an attempt to escape, it cannot regenerate it in the same way that a lizards can.

Reproduction

Worm-lizards reproduce by the males inserting their paired sex organs, known as hemipenes, into the female's cloaca to transfer sperm and achieve internal fertilization. Some species, such as the Florida worm-lizard (*Rhineura floridana*), then lay eggs that eventually hatch into small young. Eggs are sometimes laid in termite or ant nests so that the young worm-lizards have a ready supply of food when they hatch. In other species, the eggs are retained inside the mother's body until it is time for them to hatch.

Worm-Lizard Families

The commonest worm-lizards are those of the family Amphisbaenidae, whose members are found in the Mediterranean region, the Americas and Africa. The family includes the blindworm (*Blanus cinereus*) of North Africa and the Iberian peninsula, the only European species of worm-lizard, while the family Bipedidae, or Mexican worm-lizard, includes the only species to possess legs. The forelimbs are used to help the reptiles move about when above ground, and they also assist in digging through the soil. One of the most frequently encountered species is the two-legged worm-lizard (*Bipes biporus*) of Mexico, the close proximity of its front limbs in relation to its head having given rise to its

local name that translates as 'the little lizard with big ears'.

The family Rhineuridae contains only one species, the Florida worm-lizard (*Rhineura floridana*). It grows up to 16in (41cm) in length but has a diameter of only about 0.2in (0.5cm) and has a distinctly spade-shaped head. As the name suggests, it is found in Florida, but fossil evidence shows that the species was once widely dispersed across North America. It lays three eggs in a burrow. The family Rhineuridae is now often included in the family Amphisbaenidae.

Members of the final family, the Trogonophidae, are also described as edge-snouted worm-lizards because of their distinctly wedge-shaped heads bearing ridges. As they burrow, they rotate their heads in an oscillating pattern, using the specially-shaped fronts of their heads to shear off pieces of soil. The Somali edge-snout (*Agamodon*

anguliceps) of eastern Africa has a thicker, shorter body compared with that of many other species of worm-lizards, and a short, tapering tail. The front of the head is shaped like a wedge or scraper, as its name suggests, and it also bears a pair of sharp ridges. By using a twisting, screwing motion, the Somali edge-snout can excavate soil with ease to make its tunnels and can also compact the soil as it goes along. In conservation terms, worm-lizards are not at risk.

*Blindworm or worm-lizard (*Blanus cinereus*).*

CHAPTER FIVE
SNAKES

Whether gliding effortlessly along the ground, swimming in the world's oceans or climbing through the branches of trees, snakes have conquered their chosen environments with a high degree of success, for there are over 2,700 different species of snakes living today. They are found on every continent, apart from Antarctica, and have exploited almost all habitats on land and in water. No snake possesses legs – the only group of living reptiles in which this is true for all its members. Nevertheless, some of the more primitive species, such as the pythons, have retained very rudimentary rear appendages and limb girdles, proving that they are descended from limbed ancestors and lost their legs during the course of evolution.

Snakes comprise the suborder Ophidia in the order Squamata, the order that also contains the lizards. Some snakes are very small – only about 6in (15cm) or so in the case of the threadsnakes (family Leptotyphlopidae) – but the biggest species, the pythons (family Pythonidae) and the boas (family Boidae), are enormous creatures frequently measuring 20–30ft (6–9m) or

more in length, by far the longest of all living reptiles. Snakes evolved quite recently compared with other reptile groups, about 100 million years ago.

The curious, and perhaps even slightly

sinister, ways of snakes, together with the fact that some are responsible for considerable numbers of human deaths each year, have led to them being feared and persecuted almost everywhere, though paradoxically, many of

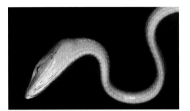

these very features have also led them to be worshipped and revered throughout history. As we shall see, snakes are indeed a fascinating group of reptiles and one that deserves to be understood and preserved rather than feared and vilified.

The main internal body parts found in other vertebrates (animals with backbones) are also present beneath the long, scaly skin of a snake, although some have become highly modified to conform to the special strictures of the snake lifestyle. First, the body length has been increased by the addition of extra spinal vertebrae, with many snakes having at least 200 vertebrae in their spinal columns and some over 400. By comparison, the human body has only 33 spinal bones. In snakes, the number of surfaces that articulate with each bone have increased to enable a greater range of movements to occur – far more than can be achieved by other vertebrates, with complicated sets of muscles responsible for moving the vertebral bones. Each vertebra carries a pair of ribs that together enclose the internal organs and provide a protective cage for them. The bones of the pectoral girdle and sternum (equivalent to the collar bones, shoulder blades and the breast bone in human

FAR LEFT
*The oriental whipsnake (*Ahaetulla prasina*) has a slim and elegant profile and is mildly venomous. Its distribution ranges from India to China and throughout South-East Asia.*

LEFT
*The blunt-headed tree snake (*Imantodes cenchoa*) photographed in Peru.*

File snakes (Mehelya sp.) are secretive and rarely seen, despite being widely distributed. They are constrictors, active at night, and prey on small vertebrates and other snakes, including venomous ones.

beings) are absent in snakes, allowing large items of food to be swallowed.

A snake's skull is also highly modified. In particular, the bones of the upper and lower jaws are only loosely connected, enabling them to move widely apart so that the reptile can swallow large prey whole. Near or at the front of a snake's jaws are a pair of curved fangs that are used to securely grip, or to kill, prey when the snake strikes. The size and arrangement of the fangs varies considerably according to the species; in venomous snakes they are used to inject poison into the victim to kill it prior to swallowing it. The rest of a snake's teeth are usually thin and sharp and point backwards to prevent prey from escaping while it is being swallowed.

The internal organs of a snake have undergone various alterations to fit the long body shape. Many have been reduced, altered in shape or repositioned, while paired lungs, seen in most vertebrates, are only present in the boas and pythons. Most other snakes have lost the left lung during the course of evolution, while the left kidney now lies behind the right, and the liver, usually a large, lobed structure in most vertebrates, is long and narrow. The females of some very thin species, such as threadsnakes, only have one oviduct. Other changes include modifications to the snake's airways, enabling it to breathe even when a large prey is lodged in its throat.

Snake Senses

As well as the senses of smell, sight, hearing, taste and touch, also present in other vertebrates, snakes also have some extra sense organs. They constantly flick their forked tongues in and out of their mouths, picking up minute scent particles in the air and on the ground. These particles are transferred to a structure called Jacobson's organ, located in

*A boomslang (*Disphodilus typus*) moving through bush on the Hwange Reserve, Zimbabwe. It is one of only two highly venomous species in the family Colubridae.*

SNAKES

the roof of the mouth, where they are analyzed and information regarding the proximity of enemies, food and, at breeding time, potential mates is extracted. Pit vipers (family Viperidae) and most boas and pythons have the ability to sense infrared heat rays, which are detected in pits on the side of the face or on the lips (these pits are the most sensitive heat detectors known in the animal kingdom). Using this apparatus, a snake can detect the minute differences in temperature between an object and its background and is so accurate that fluctuations of just a fraction of a degree can be detected, enabling the snake to home in unerringly on its prey

and to strike and catch it, even in the dark. Among the species that use this technique to detect prey are the cottonmouth (*Agkistrodon piscivorus*) of the U.S.A. and the various rattlesnake species of Canada, the U.S.A. and Mexico.

One of the most distinctive, and for many people disconcerting, features of snakes is their unblinking stare. This gives the impression that they have an even more deadly purpose, and is the result of their lack of eyelids. Instead, the eye is covered by a protective transparent window known as a brille. Some species, such as the burrowing blindsnakes, have tiny eyes that do little more

than help the snake to differentiate between conditions of light and dark. Others have well-developed eyes that are used to spot prey and focus the strike effectively. For example, a Eurasian whipsnake (*Coluber gemonensis*) will watch its prey's movements carefully, chasing or tracking it as it moves, but stopping and waiting when the prey stops. Night-hunting snakes usually have eyes with vertical, slit-like pupils that open up to gather more light in dim conditions.

Legless Locomotion

A lack of legs appears to have been no hindrance to the snake's development and the

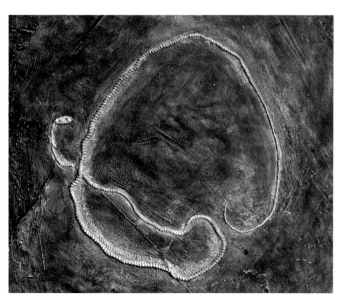

*Rainbow boa (*Epicrates cenchria*).*

Green python (Chondropython viridis). *Its coloration helps conceal it in trees.*

along eluded biologists, and several fanciful theories were postulated in an attempt to explain the phenomenon, including the theory that they 'walked' by using their ribs as a system of 'internal legs'. However, the subject has now been extensively studied and it has been found that snakes use a variety of different methods when moving. Large, heavy snakes such as pythons use a kind of 'caterpillar' movement, making use of large scales on the underside of the body. Successive groups of these scales are erected, angled in a forward direction, pressed against the ground, then pulled backward by muscles attached to the ribs, steadily levering the snake forward in a straight line. This method, known as rectilinear motion, is effective but results only in fairly slow progress, though sometimes it is used in conjunction with other methods.

FAR LEFT
Skeleton of a boa constrictor showing the large jaw gap, backward-pointing teeth and thin spines arising from each vertebra

conquest of its habitat. In fact, snakes were the last of the reptile groups to appear on earth over 70 million years ago suggesting, perhaps, that the limbless way of life was an evolutionary advance for the reptiles. Almost all snakes that are capable of moving over the ground, climbing up trees or swimming in water seem to do so with the same apparent ease, despite the fact that some are more specialized in one of these methods of locomotion. Using their special methods of locomotion, a few species can even burrow under the ground, while some snakes can move along the ground at speeds of up to 7mph (11km/h), with a few travelling even faster.

To begin with, the discovery of the mechanism by which snakes manage to move

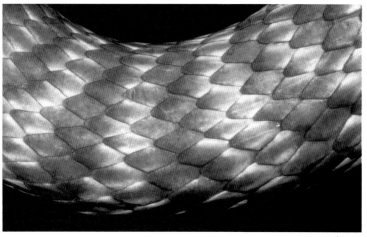

LEFT
*Detail of the skin of the coachwhip (*Masticophis flagellum*). This common snake receives its name from the braided appearance of its scales, which resemble the whip used by stagecoach drivers in earlier times.*

In another, quicker method of locomotion, a snake uses its powerful muscles to perform side-to-side undulations. As it forms its body into a series of S-shaped curves, the rear part of each curve pushes against small obstructions and any other frictional surfaces, propelling the rest of the snake forward. This is extremely effective and efficient, and the snake is able to glide forward in a smooth motion. Many snakes use this method, often in combination with rectilinear motion.

Sand can become extremely hot during the day, and snakes that live in deserts have developed a special way of coping with it. Their method of locomotion is known as sidewinding, and is the one used by species such as the American sidewinder (*Crotalus cerastes*). When sidewinding, the snake forms the front part of its body into an arc, pitching the head region forward as it does so. It then pulls the rest of the body through the arc while pitching the head forward again, the body facing at an angle to its direction of movement as it proceeds. The benefits of this method of locomotion are that only a small part of the snake's body is in contact with the hot sand at any one moment, and the snake does not need to push against the ground, which is often soft and yielding, making the more common method of progress difficult and energy-sapping. Snakes that use the sidewinding method leave a telltale 'lazy' S-shaped trail in the sand.

When climbing trees, many snakes use either rectilinear motion or the 'standard' side-to-side undulation. But some, including tree boas like the emerald tree boa (*Boa caninus*) that live in rainforests in South America, use a concertina-like method when climbing. First, they secure themselves to a branch with their prehensile tails, then they push up with the rest of the body until they reach a higher branch, securing themselves by hooking their neck around it. Finally, they release the grip with the tail and pull the rest of the body up level with the neck. A snake's long, muscular body also serves it well in the trees; by coiling its body tightly around branches it can hold itself securely while it makes a grab for food or defends itself from enemies.

As already mentioned, many snakes take readily to water in search of food and swim steadily using undulations of their bodies. But the seasnakes and seakraits (family Elapidae) are highly adapted to the marine life. Many have specially flattened tails to help them swim, and some are only able to move on land rather inefficiently. The flying snakes (*Chrysopelea* species) have even taken to gliding through the air.

How Snakes Feed

All snakes are carnivorous without exception; moreover, taking the snake order as a whole, a huge variety of different animals are eaten. Some species, like the common gartersnake (*Thamnophis sirtalis*) of North America, are extremely unspecialized in their food preferences, consuming almost anything that can be swallowed, with grasshoppers, worms, frogs, birds and small mammals like mice all contributing to their diet. Other snakes are more particular, specializing in one or just a few types of prey. The annulated seasnake (*Emydocephalus annulatus*) eats only the eggs of certain species of fish, while the red-belly snake (*Storeria occipitomaculata*) of North America feeds entirely on slugs. Many snakes

OPPOSITE
Tree snake (Leptophis sp.) with mouth wide open ready to attack.

FAR LEFT
*Skeleton of the head of a reticulated python (*Python reticulatus*), showing backward-pointing teeth.*

use one of two methods of subduing their prey prior to swallowing it, while some kill their it by constriction. It is incorrectly assumed that a constrictor crushes its prey to death, breaking all its bones in the process; in fact, it simply squeezes the victim so tightly that it is unable to expand its chest to breathe and death occurs from suffocation. The best-known constrictors are the pythons and boas, but many other snakes also kill their prey in this manner. The other method, used to great effect by the elapids and the vipers, is to inject the prey with venom to kill it first. Thus the use of constriction or injection of venom enables snakes to overpower large prey when it is encountered – although smaller prey is just as readily accepted. Snakes that have no special weapons at their disposal, other than their teeth and jaws, simply swallow their food alive.

Many constrictors are heavy-bodied,

*Like many other snakes, grass snakes (*Natrix natrix*) are capable of swimming and include aquatic creatures such as frogs and newts in their diet.*

slow-moving reptiles that lie in wait for their prey, although others actively but stealthily track their victims. These snakes usually have cryptically-coloured markings on their bodies that help them to remain concealed in trees or on the forest floor. Once prey is within range, a constrictor strikes, grabbing the prey in its teeth and holding it firmly. If the prey is too large to swallow immediately, the snake wraps a series of body coils around the victim, then squeezes with its immensely powerful muscles. As soon as the victim

breathes out, the snake tightens its grip on the body even more, preventing the victim from taking in air when it eventually suffocates. Pythons mainly feed on warm-blooded vertebrates (birds and mammals), the bigger species, like the 20-ft (6.1-m) Indian python (*Python molurus*) of India, South-East Asia and Indonesia, taking prey as large as deer and wild boar, while others will tackle predatory big cats such as leopards and will subdue and swallow crocodiles. There are even a few grizzly instances of Indian pythons

devouring human beings.

The venomous snakes, often known as the 'advanced snakes', occur mainly in three families. The first, the Colubridae or harmless snakes, include many that we would not consider dangerous, such as the grass snake (*Natrix natrix*) of Africa and Eurasia. Sometimes kept as pets, even these have a toxic secretion, although it is not harmful to human beings. The spotted watersnake (*Enhydris punctata*) of Australia is also mildly poisonous, using its venom to subdue

fish and frogs. However, the members of the family Elapidae, or front-fanged snakes, are a different matter altogether. All the members of this family are venomous, and some truly deadly species are included, such as the 5-ft (1.5-m) long eastern brown snake (*Pseudonaja textilis*) of Australia – one of the world's most lethal snakes – and the 18-ft (5.5-m) long king cobra (*Ophiophagus hannah*) of Asia. The vipers or Viperidae belong to the other family of highly venomous snakes, which include several American species such as the diamondback rattlesnakes (*Crotalus* species), the sidewinder (*Crotalus cerastes*) and the cottonmouth (*Agkistrodon piscivorus*). Many venomous snakes have bright warning coloration to advertise the fact and deter would-be predators, though other harmless species occasionally mimic their body patterns to avoid being attacked.

Specially modified teeth, known as fangs, are used to pierce the victim's skin before the poison is injected. There are three types of fang arrangement in snakes: first, there are back-fanged snakes, like the African boomslang (*Dispholidus typus*) in the family Colubridae. As the name suggests, back-fanged snakes have small fangs situated towards the backs of their mouths, with special grooves through which the venom runs before it is injected. The front-fanged snakes, like the cobras, have longer, more tubular fangs situated nearer the front of the mouth down which venom flows. Finally, the vipers, such as the eastern diamondback rattlesnakes (*Crotalus adamanteus*), have fangs at the front of the mouth which can be

*An African mole snake (*Pseudaspis cana*) emerging from its burrow in the Kalahari Gemsbok National Park, South Africa. These spend most of their time underground searching for prey, which includes rats, moles and other small mammals.*

A colubrid snake in leaf litter in rainforest in Tobago. Although most are venomous, they are harmless to human beings.

The Madagascan tree boa (Sanzinia madagascariensis) is mainly green to greyish-green in colour. The young are born a reddish-brown and acquire the adult green colour within the first year. However, a yellowish form, known as the 'mandarin' phase, occurs in some parts of Madagascar.

lungs have ceased to work. Haemotoxins have a different effect on the body: they break down tissues such as red and white blood cells and disrupt the normal working of the blood-clotting mechanisms in the body. Snake venom is a cocktail of both neurotoxins and haemotoxins, working in conjunction with one another to do their deadly work; sometimes the venom produces a range of symptoms that act together to bring about the death of the prey. Other substances in the venom include enzymes which help the venom to spread more quickly.

Curiously, because snake venom is essentially a protein, it needs to enter the

'folded away' inside fleshy tissue when not in use. As the snake strikes, the fangs swing forward, ready for action. Snakes never inject more than half their supply of venom in one bite, and more is manufactured in the snake's body once it has been used.

It is likely that snake venom evolved from the digestive juices as it is usually produced in glands located in the upper jaw or near the sides of the head, but a few species produce venom in long, tubular glands extending into the body. The highly venomous snakes, such as the cobras and vipers, have relatively larger spaces set aside for venom storage than other, less dangerous species. Snake venom is a colourless to amber fluid containing biologically-active proteins. These are mainly substances known as neurotoxins, but haemotoxins are also present. Neurotoxins work by blocking nerve impulses to the victim's muscles and causing paralysis, with death usually occurring because the heart and

OPPOSITE

*A boomslang (*Dispholidus typus*) on* Berzelia lanuginosa *on Table Mountain, Cape Town, South Africa.*

LEFT

*A cape cobra (*Naja nivea*) raiding a weaver's nest for chicks. It injects its prey with a neurotoxic venom which causes the rapid onset on paralysis.*

LEFT

*A rosy boa (*Lichanura trivirgata*) eating a mouse. It is most active at dusk and at night and feeds largely on small mammals and birds, which it kills by constriction. If attacked by a predator, the boa rolls up into a ball, keeping its head in the centre, and releases a foul-smelling musk from the base of its tail.*

An olive seasnake (Aipysurus laevis) on the seabed, where it feeds on fish eggs.

SNAKES

bloodstream directly to be effective. Therefore, it has little effect if swallowed. This is the reason why snakes are not killed by their own venom when swallowing a victim they have recently injected – and also why it is safe to suck out the poison from a snake bite to save a person's life. Cobras have the most venom, the king cobra having enough to kill an elephant. Over 50 different species of venomous snakes have been implicated in attacks on human beings, with effects ranging from fairly mild pain and discomfort to death. It is estimated that about 40,000 people worldwhile are killed each year in this manner.

After a snake has subdued or despatched its victim by one of the methods just described, it must find a way of dealing with it. The teeth of snakes are not designed for chewing or biting pieces off, so anything a snake eats must be swallowed whole. Relatively small items, such as worms or slugs, present no problems, but how does a snake cope with a prey many times wider than its own head and body – a zebra or a crocodile, for example? The skull of a snake is unlike that of any other vertebrate in that

SNAKES

*The drab skin pattern of the anaconda (*Eunectes murinus*) ensures that it blends in well with the wet, dense vegetation of its habitat. It is the largest snake in the world.*

the bones in the top half of the jaw can move independently and are only fixed to the skull bones by ligaments and muscles. The front of the lower jaw bones are also only connected to one another loosely. Furthermore, the upper and lower jaws of a snake are not fixed to one another in the same way as they are in other vertebrates. The jaw hinge is set further back, behind the skull, giving the snake a

gigantic gape when it fully opens its mouth.

To consume a large item of food, the snake usually turns its victim round so that it can be swallowed head-first. There are several reasons for this: first, the victim may still be alive, and by starting at the head the snake reduces the likelihood of it retaliating. Second, the victim's limbs will be pushed back along the sides of its body if it is

ingested in this way, making it easier to swallow. Prey such as other reptiles or fish are also simpler to swallow if the edges of the scales are facing backwards. As the snake swallows its victim, it uses the highly mobile jaws to stretch and 'walk' over the prey, at the same time utilizing its backward-pointing teeth to force the meal down. During this process, the upper and lower halves of the jaw also move apart to an astonishing degree, allowing surprisingly large and bulky items to be accommodated. The skin of the snake's head, throat and body is also flexible, allowing it to stretch as the food goes down; needless to say, swallowing a large meal can be a lengthy process. Once the food is safely in the stomach, however, the snake can retreat to a quiet place to digest it. The outline of the animal that a snake has consumed is usually clearly visible, distending the snake's normally elongated outline into one that is much bulkier and more irregular. Snakes have slow metabolisms and do not need to eat very often, with many eating once a week or even less, while a large snake, such as a python, may get by on one good meal a year.

Eggs form part of the diet of many snakes, favourite choices being small eggs, particularly soft-shelled ones belonging to snakes and lizards, since snakes can cope with them and slit them open with their teeth. However, larger, calcareous shelled birds' eggs are another matter, and to deal with them requires special body adaptations. The egg-eating snake (*Dasypeltis scabra*) of African woodland and scrub is one such specialist. This slender reptile hunts for eggs on the ground and in trees, and when it finds a

The western diamondback rattlesnake (Crotalus atrox) is one of the most venomous snakes in the U.S.A. The rattle on the end of the tail serves to warn off intruders; after each moult, the rattle gains a new section as the last scale loosens but fails to fall off.

suitable one, begins to 'walk' its jaws over the egg, gradually engulfing it, the ridges on the sides of the mouth helping to prevent the slippery egg from sliding out of its mouth. As with other snakes, the jaws of the egg-eating snake can extend to surround the egg, and the flexible skin stretches to facilitate swallowing

it. Eventually, the egg, perhaps several times bigger than the snake's head, is inside the body. Now the snake uses its muscles to push special inward-projecting spines on its backbone against the eggshell in order to break it, the contents of the egg pass into the snake's stomach, and the shell is regurgitated.

Because the egg-eating snake almost immediately discards the shell, the stomach does not hold superfluous material for long. This means that it can eat as many eggs as it can find, enabling it to build up a store of fat to tide it over during seasons when eggs are not as plentiful.

Social Behaviour and Mating

Snakes in temperate regions usually hibernate over winter. During this time, food is scarce or even absent, and the temperature often drops too low for the body to function normally. Many snakes gather together with others of their own species to spend the cold months in a safe hole somewhere out of the way. With the onset of spring, however, the snakes wake from their hibernation and congregate outside their den, often en masse, to bask in the sunshine. A dormant period of inactivity may be seen in snakes that live in the tropics, but in this instance they use this dormancy to avoid the dry season. One of the first activities that a snake engages in following hibernation is skin-shedding, when last year's old skin is rubbed off, revealing a new skin underneath. This is an important period for a snake, for the appearance of new skin also coincides with growth.

In mature female snakes, moulting of the skin also triggers a hormone that lets males know they are ready to mate. Apart from those snakes that hibernate together, most individuals lead solitary lives. However, at mating time snakes may gather in large numbers, and for reptiles that hardly seem to notice one another most of the time, there is a sudden surge of interest in others of their kind. Eager male suitors may cluster around a mature female, with rivals often engaging in a kind of combat dance or pushing contest as they vie for the right to mate with her. These contests may sometimes last for an hour or more until the successful male eventually approaches the female and stimulates her to mate by placing his chin on her neck while rubbing himself along the length of her body. The rear parts of their bodies may become entwined as they prepare to mate. At this time, some males grasp the female's neck in their mouths, and boas and pythons use their spurs – in reality the remains of the pelvic girdle – to rub the female's cloacal region. If

An eastern hog-nosed snake (Heterodon platyrhinos) *shedding its skin.*

*Adders (*Vipera berus*) prior to mating.*

OPPOSITE
*Adder (*Vipera berus*).*

LEFT
A female adder having just given birth. Adders have quite variable skin patterns, as seen here.

the female accepts the male, she lifts her tail so that he can insert one of his hemipenes into her cloaca. In a few species, mating takes place late in the year and the male's sperm may then be stored in special parts of the female's oviduct known as spermathecae. She then waits until the following spring before allowing the sperm from the spermathecae to fertilize the eggs; sperm may occasionally be stored for up to four years in this way before fertilization takes place.

Once mating has occurred, the snakes resume their separate lives, the female, in egg-laying species, looking for somewhere to deposit her eggs. The sites chosen are varied, but favourite places are in soil under rocks, in decomposing compost or among rotting logs; whichever site is chosen, it needs to be damp and warm as cold or wet conditions prevent the eggs from incubating. In most cases, once the eggs have been laid, the female departs to leave them to their fate. But a few species actively guard their eggs to prevent predators from stealing them, a form of behaviour most often seen in the pythons, Some females curl around their eggs and guard them until they have hatched. In tropical climates, this behaviour is unlikely to be associated with keeping the eggs warm, although in cooler, temperate climates the female may assist with incubation by using the warmth of her body. Some species, such as carpet pythons (*Calabaria reinhardtii*), even move away from their eggs for a time to bask in the sun and warm their bodies so that they may brood the eggs more efficiently. The female king cobra (*Ophiophagus hannah*) builds a mound nest using twigs, leaves and soil, in the top of

which she forms a cavity into which to deposit her eggs. She then covers them with more leaves and material before curling up on top of the mound to stand guard until the eggs hatch.

Egg-laying species are to be found among the pythons (family Pythonidae), the blindsnakes (family Typhlopidae), the harmless snakes (family Colubridae), the front-fanged snakes (family Elapidae) and the vipers (family Viperidae), although most of these also have members that produce live young. The number of eggs laid varies widely according to the species: the common kingsnake (*Lampropeltis getulus*) of the U.S.A. and Mexico usually lays between three and 24 eggs; the Indian cobra (*Naja naja*) produces up to 45 eggs; and the Indian python (*Python molurus*) lays up to 100 eggs. Incubation time also varies, but is normally between four weeks and four months.

Live-bearing snakes retain their eggs inside the body until they hatch, giving birth to live young. The females of one or two species of live-bearers even develop a placenta, similar to the one found in mammals. (The placenta is an organ consisting of blood-rich tissues that are used to nourish the developing embryos with food from the mother.) The level of maternal care afforded to the hatchlings of, say, crocodilians, is not as evident in snakes. However, a few species, such as asp vipers (*Vipera aspis*), guard their young for a short time after they are born.

The speed at which the young snakes grow depends upon how much food is available. Snakes that hatch in the fall in temperate regions may not eat until the

following spring, after their winter hibernation, therefore no growth will occur until then. Some snakes in warmer climates may get the chance to eat almost as soon as they hatch, and in these species growth may be rapid and they may double in size within four months. Usually, snakes do most of their growing within the first five years of life, by which time they are sexually mature. Growth may then slow down although, in the right conditions, snakes continue to grow, albeit very slowly, for the rest of their lives, which may last for 20 years or more. This helps to explain the enormous variation in the sizes of snakes of the same species, with occasional giants still being recorded despite so much destruction of their habitat.

SNAKE FAMILIES
The suborder Ophidia is divided into 11 families which can be further grouped into three categories: primitive snakes; blindsnakes; advanced snakes. The four families of primitive snakes are so-called because they display a number of features that suggest that they are closely related to lizards or lizard-like ancestors. These include the arrangement of the bony plates, or scutes, found on the underside of the body and the head, and the possession in primitive examples of vestiges of the hindlimbs, visible as spur-like structures on the sides of the cloacal opening. In the lower jaw, all primitive snakes have an extra bone called the coronoid, and most species have retained two lungs, whereas in the other groups the left lung has been lost, making the body more streamlined.

The four families of blindsnakes are even

OPPOSITE
The adder is the only venomous snake in Britain.

more unlike typical snakes. Some scientists think their features point to them being highly primitive, while others suggest that they are simply highly adapted to their burrowing lifestyle. Whichever is true, the earthworm-like blindsnakes certainly followed a different route at some point during the evolution of snakes. The majority of them show some of the same primitive features displayed by the family Pythonidae, such as remains of the pelvis and retention of the coronoid, but the teeth are also noticeably absent and so is the left lung. In addition, the skull bones have become fused to form a tough battering structure for burrowing through soil. The eyes are tiny, since eyesight is not an essential sense for living in darkness below ground, and are hidden behind bony plates. Since blindsnakes do not use the same methods of locomotion adopted by their above-ground relatives, the bony scutes of the underside of the body are absent, having instead been replaced by scales of the type found on the top of the body. The mouth is also small, since the food of most blindsnakes consists of nothing larger than earthworms, ants and termites. They are subdivided into the big-jaw blindsnakes and the weak-jaw blindsnakes, the maxillary bone being fused to the skull in the former, while in the weak-jaw the maxilla is movable.

Over 80 per cent of all snakes belong to the group known as the advanced snakes. In these, only the right lung is used and not one of the three families that make up the group have any sign of the pelvic girdle or the coronoid bone. It is also within the advanced snakes that we see the wide use of venom rather than constriction as a means of subduing prey.

It is worth noting that the snake family tree has been revised by various taxonomists, and in doing so a few little-known species of snakes have now been removed from their original families and placed in newly created ones, often consisting of one or two members only. These include the two species of Asian sunbeam snakes of the family Xenopeltidae found in South-East Asia and the East Indies, the Mexican burrowing python or neotropical sunbeam snake (*Loxocemus bicolor*) of the family Loxocemidae, found in Mexico and Central America, and the 60 or so species of stiletto snakes in the family Atractaspididae, located in sub-Saharan Africa and the Arabian peninsula. In such new systems of classification, up to 18 families of snakes may be recognized in total, instead of the 11 described in this book.

FAMILY PYTHONIDAE

The family Pythonidae, one of the families of primitive snakes, contains about 27 species. They are found throughout many parts of the tropics from Mexico, Central America, sub-Saharan Africa, India, South-East Asia, the East Indies and Australia, where they inhabit scrub, bush and rainforest. Birds and mammals form the major part of their diet, and some of the largest species take animals as big as deer and even leopards, with other reptiles sometimes becoming meals for pythons. In terms of size, pythons range from the Australian children's python (*Liasis childreni*), which is only about 3-ft (0.9-m) long, to giants like the reticulated python

(*Python reticulatus*) of South-East Asia, often measuring up to 33ft (10m). A reticulated python captured recently in Sumatra measured a staggering 49ft (15m) from nose to tail-tip, probably making it the longest snake ever captured. Most, however, are about 10–20-ft (3–6-m) long. Pythons are masters of the art of constriction, first grabbing prey with their teeth and then wrapping their thick, muscular body coils around the victim, squeezing it until it suffocates. All pythons lay eggs.

A typical mid-sized example is the carpet python (*Morelia spilotes*) of Australia and New Guinea. This widely-distributed snake is found in forest and scrub, where its brown and gold patterning helps it mimic dead leaves. The carpet python moves as effectively in water and in trees as it does on the ground. By day it usually rests among trees or on the ground, while at night it seeks out mice, rabbits and birds, which it first ensnares with its sharp teeth before wrapping them in its deadly coils.

The Indian python (*Python molurus*) is a large python measuring about 20ft (6m) in length. It is a thick-bodied snake with attractive, reticulated patterning on its skin. Heat sensors located near its nostrils help it to track down its prey, which consists mainly of mice, birds, deer and wild boar. By day it basks in the sun or rests up in caves, burrows or similar locations, and at night hunts for food, often by waterholes.

Some pythons have evolved a burrowing lifestyle. The sunbeam python (*Xenopeltis unicolor*) of South-East Asia has no vestiges of hindlimbs – an unusual feature for a primitive snake. It gets its common name from the hues produced by its smooth, iridescent blue scales. It feeds on frogs, rodents and birds. The Mexican burrowing python (*Loxocemus bicolor*) is found along the Pacific coast from Mexico to Costa Rica and is the only python found in the Americas. The other burrowing python is the Calabar python (*Calabaria reinhardtii*), found in West Africa. If disturbed, it wraps its head in a ball of body coils.

Conservation status: six species are Critically Endangered; seven are Endangered; eight are classed as Vulnerable.

*The African python (*Python sebae*) is the largest snake in Africa. It feeds on prey as large as impala.*

FAMILY ANILIIDAE

The second family of primitive snakes, the family Aniliidae or pipesnakes, consists of 11 species. They are found in the Amazon basin region of South America, in Burma, Indo-China and the East Indies. Pipesnakes are burrowers, specializing in attacking and consuming underground reptiles such as other burrowing snakes and amphisbaenids. Their length is up to 3ft (0.9mm). The Asian pipesnakes burrow into damp soil and often frequent rice paddy fields and swamps. They are normally black in colour. The false coral snake or coral pipesnake (*Anilius scytale*) is found in forests in northern South America, east of the Andes Mountains. Its body is brightly marked with alternating bands of black and red, mimicking those often seen in venomous snakes, such as the eastern coral snake (*Micrurus fulvius*). The false coral snake has a small head and tiny eyes that are hidden beneath transparent scales. The young develop inside the female's body and are born fully formed.

FAMILY TROPIDOPHIIDAE

Another family of primitive snakes, the Tropidophiidae, are also known as protocolubroids. Their distribution includes the West Indies, Mexico, parts of South America and Round Island in the Indian Ocean. The maximum size realized by these species is usually about 2ft (0.6m). In colour, most species are brownish, with darker markings or lighter bands, and the body is large in proportion to the head on which there are large scutes of the type found in the advanced snakes. Another 'advanced' feature

OPPOSITE
*The reticulated python (*Python reticulatus*).*

LEFT
An African python consuming a whole antelope.

is the elongated hyoid bone in the throat and the possession of only one lung. The woodsnakes are found in Mexico and South America, although they are more common in the West Indies. Secretive and essentially nocturnal, they hunt out small lizards and mammals to eat.

Round Island, in the Indian Ocean, is the last refuge of two other species, the Round Island snake (*Bolyeria multocarinata*) and the Round Island keel-scaled snake (*Casarea dussumieri*), although they were once also found on nearby Mauritius. Uniquely, in these two snakes, the maxillary bone of the upper jaw is divided into two parts. Little is known of these two rare snakes, and it is quite possible that the Round Island snake has even become extinct. Both have been placed in a new family, the family Bolyeriidae or split-jaw boas, by some taxonomists.

FAMILY BOIDAE

The last of the families of primitive snakes, the Boidae or boas, contain some of the largest of all living snakes. There are 39 species in this widely-distributed family, which ranges from western North America,

*Emerald tree boa (*Corallus caninus*).*

Central America and the Caribbean, throughout many parts of South America, much of the northern part of Africa, Madagascar, the Middle East, western Asia and New Guinea. Some members are tree-dwellers, some are terrestrial and others are mainly aquatic. Most boas are about 6.5–13ft (2–4m) in length, but among the giants of the family are the boa constrictors (*Boa constrictor*) of Mexico, Central and South America and the anaconda (*Eunectes murinus*). The boa constrictor grows to about 18ft (5.5m), while the anaconda reaches lengths in excess of 36ft (11m). Boas have

slender, muscular bodies and long tails. The head is often relatively small, but is distinctive and almost dog-like. It bears heat-sensing pits on the lips that are used to   detect warm-bodied prey, killing them by constriction. All boas are live-bearers, and some species give birth to as many as 80 young.

One of the best-known of the arboreal boas is the emerald tree boa (*Boa caninus*), found in rainforests in parts of South America such as Guyana and Brazil. About 4-ft (1.2-m) long, this beautifully marked green snake spends much of its life in the trees waiting for prey such as birds and small mammals to

appear. It is a fast-moving species that can also swim well. The boa constrictor, the second largest species of snake in the Americas, is found in a wide range of habitats that include deserts and rainforests. Primarily a ground-dweller, the boa constrictor can also climb trees and hunts birds and mammals. The huge anaconda is found in South America as far south as Argentina, where it lives in swampy river valleys. Its method of hunting is to lurk in murky shallow water waiting for unsuspecting animals to come to drink, but it also eats aquatic turtles and caimans. The

*Anaconda (*Eunectes murinus*), photographed in Hato el Cedral, Venezuela.*

SNAKES

OPPOSITE

The anaconda is a huge species that can grow to 36ft (11m) or more.

anaconda can remain concealed beneath the water surface for some time, but usually floats along with just the top of its head visible. Some West Indian boas (*Epicrates* species) lurk in caves and feed on bats.

Unlike other boas, the rubber boa (*Charina bottae*) ranges far into the temperate zone. A relatively small species, at about 30in (76cm) in length, this snake is found in the western U.S.A. from Washington down to California in a range of different habitats including forests, meadows and riversides. The rubber boa is usually active at dusk and at night, when it searches out small birds, mammals and lizards. It is a species that can climb well with the help of its prehensile tail. During the day the snake takes refuge under logs or rocks or burrows into soft soil. The female produces up to eight live young in late summer.

Conservation status: two species are classed as Endangered; four are Vulnerable.

FAMILY UROPELTIDAE

The shield-tail snakes of the family Uropeltidae, of which there are about 45 species, are members of the group known as the big-jaw blindsnakes, all of which are burrowing reptiles found in damp hillsides in India and Sri Lanka. They get their name from the distinctive scutes covering the upper surface of the tail. Shield-tails are usually between 8–20in (20–51cm) in length, although a few are a little bigger. Their long, cylindrical bodies are iridescent black or brown, frequently marked with bright-red, yellow or white patches. The red-blotched

shield-tail (*Uropeltis bimaculatus*) of India and Sri Lanka is about 12-in (30.5-cm) long. It feeds on earthworms and grubs which it hunts underground, moving by forming its body into a series of S-shapes, pressing them against the tunnel sides, then thrusting its head into the soil. The female gives birth to up to eight young that develop inside her body. Blyth's landau shield-tail (*Rhinophis blythii*) of Sri Lanka burrows in the soil using the same technique as the red-blotched shield-tail and feeds on earthworms. It also gives birth to live fully-formed young.

FAMILY LEPTOTYPHLOPIDAE

The second of the big-jaw blindsnake families, the threadsnakes are small, worm-shaped burrowers, of which there are about 90 species distributed in the south-west U.S.A., Central America, South America, the Bahamas, Africa (except the Sahara Desert), and east through Saudi Arabia to Pakistan. The head is reduced in size and there are teeth in the lower jaws only, which since these snakes eat only ants and termites does not present a problem. Body colours are grey, blackish or pink. Their tiny eyes are concealed beneath scales, reflecting their underground lifestyle. The western blindsnake (*Leptotyphlops humilis*) ranges from south-west U.S.A. to Mexico, where it lives in arid conditions. It is pinkish with a smooth body and a blunt head and tail and measures about 15in (38cm). It burrows in sandy or gravelly soil, spending most of its life underground feeding on ants and termites, though in humid conditions or when nights are warm it may sometimes emerge.

Like other threadsnakes, the western blindsnake lays eggs.

FAMILY ANOMALEPIDAE

The Anomalepidae, or the dawn blindsnakes, are one of the two families of weak-jaw blindsnakes. There are about 20 species in the family, all of which are found in Central and South America. They are mainly brown or black in colour with the typical worm-like bodies of the blindsnakes, and have indistinct heads and short tails. They spend much of their time buried under leaf litter or burrowed in soil in rainforests. Termites and similar small invertebrates form the bulk of their diet.

FAMILY TYPHLOPIDAE

Members of the second of the two families of weak-jaw blindsnakes, the Typhlopidae are also referred to as typical blindsnakes. There are over 200 species in the family, which has a wide distribution in warm to temperate and tropical regions of the world. They are found in Mexico, the Bahamas, South America, Africa south of the Sahara Desert, south-eastern Europe to southern Asia and Australia. The largest grow to about 3ft (0.9m) in length, but most are smaller – about 8–20-in (20–51-cm) long. Colours range from brown, black, pink or yellow, suffused with blotches or bands depending on the species. The cylindrical body has smooth, polished scales and the small head bears no teeth in the lower jaw. They inhabit grassland, scrub and rainforest, where they burrow below ground to feed on termites, ants and insect larvae. Some members are egg-layers, while others give birth to live young. One of the best-

FAR RIGHT

*A grass snake (*Natrix natrix*) swimming, while flicking out its tongue, possibly to catch the flies which have landed on its head. When threatened, this species emits a foul-smelling liquid from its anal glands. If this fails, it will roll onto its back and play dead until the attacker loses interest.*

OPPOSITE

*An oriental whipsnake (*Ahaetulla prasina*), photographed in the Bako National Park, Sarawak.*

known members of the family is Schlegel's blindsnake (*Typhlops schlegelii*), a large species found in Africa. It has a spine on the end of its tail that helps it to burrow by providing leverage. The female of this species lays up to 60 eggs. The tiny flowerpot snake (*Rhamphotyphlops braminus*) has a wide distribution because it has been introduced into many parts of the world by accident, having become a 'stowaway' in the soil of nursery plants that originated in tropical and subtropical countries – hence its common name.

Conservation status: one species is Endangered; one species is Vulnerable.

FAMILY COLUBRIDAE

This family is one of the three groups known as advanced snakes. About 1,760 species make up the family Colubridae or the colubrids – by far the largest family of snakes in terms of numbers. The family is also referred to as that of the harmless snakes because most of its members do not produce venom of sufficient toxicity to be a problem to human beings. In the colubrids there are no species with hollow poison fangs as there are in the other families of advanced snakes, the elapids and vipers. Instead, venom from the poison gland flows along grooves in the teeth at the rear of the mouth. As might be expected of such a huge family, the range of sizes is enormous: the smallest species are only a few inches long, but the largest grow to nearly 12ft (3.7m) in length. The colubrids are widely distributed, appearing on all continents apart from Antarctica. Their range extends

RIGHT
*Grass snake (*Natrix natrix*).*

OPPOSITE
*Green vine snake (*Oxybelis
fulgidus*). The long, thin body
resembles the lianas and vines that
festoon the trees of its habitat,
helping it to remain concealed.*

from the Arctic circle in Scandinavia and Siberia south to the tips of South America and South Africa and as far as north-east Australia. They are, however, absent from a few oceanic islands such as New Zealand. Colubrids are found everywhere from desert to rainforest, and they have exploited most habitats under the ground, on the ground, in trees and in water. Several of the colubrid species are kept as pet snakes, but despite their generally non-aggressive natures some may still bite painfully on occasions.

The family Colubridae is a somewhat convenient collection of broadly similar species, but its sheer diversity and size means that it is often subdivided into smaller subfamilies in which the relationships between the individual species are easier to discern. One widely-used system divides the colubrid into six subfamilies. The first group, the Ethiopian snakes, are found in scrub and rainforests in tropical zones. Most occur in sub-Saharan Africa and Madagascar, though a few live in South-East Asia. The neotropical snakes inhabit tropical rainforests as well as arid scrub and occur mainly in the New World, although some appear in North America. The next group contains the aquatic wartsnakes of Asia. The watersnakes and gartersnakes are also aquatic or semi-aquatic and are found in many parts of the Northern Hemisphere, Central America, Asia and Australia. Racers and rat snakes are mainly distributed in the Northern Hemisphere, but also occur in South America, Africa, South-East Asia and Australia. Finally, the sand snakes live in grassland and semi-desert mainly in Africa but also in southern Europe and Asia.

OPPOSITE
*A captive specimen of the tiger rat snake (*Spilotes pullatus*) at La Selva Biological Reserve, Costa Rica. This arboreal tropical species feeds on lizards, birds, and mammals as large as squirrels.*

LEFT
*Gopher snake (*Pituophis melanoleucus*). This species lives in all four North American deserts.*

SNAKES

A book of this size can only include descriptions of a few of the many species in the family, but it is hoped that the following accounts will help to paint a picture of their range and diversity. The slugsnakes (*Pareas* species) of South-East Asia are slender-bodied with broad heads. They inhabit forests where they feed on molluscs, their lower jaws having become especially adapted for extracting snails from their shells. At night, the snakes search out their prey and once a snail has been seized, the slugsnake extends its lower jaw into the snail's shell and fastens onto the soft body with its curved teeth. The jaw is then retracted, pulling the snail out of its shell. A similar strategy is adopted by the snail-eating snake (*Dipsas indica*) of tropical South American forests. However, a mollusc

OPPOSITE
*The gartersnake (*Thamnophis sirtalis*) is a common species throughout North America. It is found in a wide range of habitats including meadows, marshes and woodlands and along streams. Its diet varies according to its habitat, but is typically fish, frogs, earthworms, toads and sometimes small mammals, baby birds and lizards.*

FAR LEFT and BELOW
*Pike-headed vine snake (*Oxybelis aeneus).*

bellied mangrove snake (*Fordonia leucobalia*) of Australia and Asia has similar adaptations for an aquatic life, one spent hunting around the roots of mangroves that grow in swamps.

The common gartersnake (*Thamnophis sirtalis*) of North America frequents damp places such as water meadows, ditches and marshes, as well as fields and woods. This is the most widely distributed snake in North America, and many subspecies with varying coloration are found over its huge range, although most bear the distinctive stripes on the back and sides that characterize the species. Active by day, the gartersnake hunts for amphibians such as salamanders, frogs and toads, as well as invertebrates that live in damp vegetation. Because it has such a wide distribution, its habits vary according to the location and climate. In the south of its range it is normally active all year, but in the colder northern limits it hibernates in winter in company with others of its kind. Up to 80 young develop inside the female's body, nourished through a placenta. This species makes a popular pet.

One of the most common snakes in Europe and elsewhere is the grass snake (*Natrix natrix*), a species which is also well-adapted to a life in water and which is found close to marshes and streams as well as in damp meadows. Many have been alarmed to find a grass snake swimming in their garden pond, attempting to help itself to the local inhabitants! Females tend to be bigger than males, and occasionally specimens can reach 6ft (1.8m) or so in length. Most of the grass snake's diet of newts, frogs, toads, small mammals, like mice and shrews, and birds is

OPPOSITE and LEFT
*A tree snake from South Africa, the boomslang (*Dispholidus typus*) has a distinctive head, with very large eyes and black fangs. Its excellent vision helps it to hunt prey, which consists of small vertebrates, especially chameleons and birds. When cornered, it will inflate its neck to expose brightly-coloured skin.*

being attacked by the snail-eating snake produces huge quantities of mucus which is capable of clogging the snake's airways and preventing it from breathing. Therefore, the snake uses air stored in its lungs while it is tackling its meal.

The unusual-looking elephant-trunk snake (*Acrochordus javanicus*) of India and Asia is one of the wartsnakes. About 5ft (1.5m) in length, this stout, grey-coloured snake does indeed resemble an elephant's trunk, the effect enhanced by the loose, sagging skin of the body and the very tapered tail. Wartsnakes are highly adapted for swimming, so much so that they are awkward and sluggish on land. When diving, flaps in the roof of the mouth close off the airways to

prevent water from entering. Wartsnakes usually inhabit freshwater rivers and streams, where they feed mainly on fish, but sometimes they take to the sea and have been known to travel as far as Australia.

There are many aquatic species in the family Colubridae. Another is the spotted watersnake (*Enhydris punctata*) of Australian creeks and swamps. About 20-in (51-cm) long and attractively marked with reddish, blotched skin, the slightly venomous spotted watersnake basks on the river banks but slips into the water to hunt fish, frogs and other aquatic creatures. Its eyes and nostrils are situated high on its head, and flaps of skin close the nostrils when it dives. The female gives birth to fully-formed young. The white-

*An oriental whipsnake (*Ahaetulla prasina*) photographed in the Bako National Park, Sarawak.*

swallowed whole. Moreover, the grass snake has a venomous secretion that can be used to subdue its natural prey but which is harmless to human beings. The female lays about 30 or 40 eggs in a place where there is warm, decaying material such as in a compost or manure heap, and the young hatch after one or two months.

Bibron's burrowing viper, or the southern stiletto snake (*Atractaspis bibroni*) of South Africa, inhabits dry, sandy places, where it tunnels into soil using its shovel-shaped head. It has a dark, slender body, no discernible neck, a short tail and small eyes. Due to its lifestyle, it belongs to a group of burrowing colubrids known as mole vipers, and is a truly venomous colubrid, with a system of venom delivery similar to that of the true vipers; indeed, once it was believed to be one. It has large fangs that pump poison from venom glands into its victim, which is usually a blindsnake or a burrowing lizard. Bibron's burrowing viper and its relatives are sometimes placed in a separate family, the family Atractaspididae.

The rat snake (*Elaphe obsoleta*) of Canada, the U.S.A. and Mexico lives in forests, swamps and farmland. About 8-ft (2.4-m) long, this powerful creature exists as several subspecies, each of which has different patterning on its skin; some may be blotched, some striped and others plain. The rat snake is a good climber and also hunts for prey around barns and disused buildings. Prey consists mainly of rodents, birds and lizards. It is usually active by day but may also be nocturnal.

The gopher snake (*Pituophis melanoleucus*), like the rat snake, ranges south from Canada, through the U.S.A. and down to Mexico, where it prefers dry woods, prairies and deserts. It is a large, sturdy species between 4–8ft (1.2–2.4 m) in length and has a somewhat triangular-shaped head. The body usually features black, reddish or brown markings on a paler background, although colours vary across its large range. The gopher snake is normally active by day, but in very hot weather it may resort to burrowing underground for shelter, only emerging to hunt at night. Prey consists of reptiles such as lizards, birds, and mammals such as rabbits and rodents. The snake uses constriction to kill its victim, gripping it tightly in body coils until it suffocates. Like some of its relatives, the gopher can become aggressive if alarmed, first vibrating its tail rapidly and hissing before it coils and strikes. Gopher snakes lay their eggs in burrows or beneath logs or rocks, the young hatching about ten weeks later.

Not much thicker than a person's finger, the vine snakes are an extremely long, slender species that are superbly adapted for hiding in vegetation. Their long, green or green-brown bodies are almost indistinguishable from the vines and creepers that festoon the trees they inhabit – even their heads are long and thin. The vine snake (*Oxybelis fulgidus*) is found in Central and South America, and its method of hunting mainly involves raiding birds' nests to snatch nestlings, or grabbing lizards. Although mildly venomous, its main form of defence is to rear up and puff out the front of its body, revealing its bright colours. It may also open its mouth wide in a threatening display.

The boomslang (*Dispholidus typus*) of the African savanna is one of only a very few species of colubrids that are dangerously venomous. The snake grows up to 6.5ft (2m) in length, and inhabits trees where its green, brown or blackish upper surface helps it to remain concealed among the branches. It has extremely toxic venom, delivered from fangs set further forward in its mouth than most other colubrids. The venom quickly overcomes lizards, frogs and birds, but it can also cause breathing failure and haemorrhaging in humans, and even death.

This family includes the egg-eating snakes (*Dasypeltis* species), whose novel way of feeding is described on page 278. It also includes the remarkable tree snakes (*Chrysopelea* species). The paradise tree snake (*Chrysopelea paradisii*) lives in forests in South-East Asia. Up to 4-ft (1.2-m) long and with a blackish body marked with red spots, the snake has several adaptations for a life in the trees. First, it has ridged scales on its belly that help it to climb up vertical tree trunks with ease, consequently, it can reach the top branches of trees that many other snakes never venture near, and can feast on lizards without competition. But the snake's other unusual feature is its ability to fly through the air. To do this, it leaps from a branch, then flattens its body, forming it into a series of S-shapes and effectively creating a flight surface that enables it to glide. Using this technique, the paradise tree snake can perform an angled glide downwards for 60ft (18m) or more and land safely on another branch. Other tree snakes in the genus can glide in a similar manner.

FAR RIGHT

*The green mamba (*Dendroaspis angusticeps*) is a highly venomous arboreal cobra. It kills its victims by injecting a neurotoxin which prevents breathing. Eventually, the heart stops.*

Conservation status: one species, the St. Croix racer (*Alsophis sancticrucis*) of the Virgin Islands, is now considered to be extinct.

FAMILY ELAPIDAE

This is the second family in the group of advanced snakes. The family Elapidae are all front-fanged snakes; the short, tubular fangs are situated near the front of the mouth and deliver fast-acting, highly potent venom that usually disrupts the nervous system. Because of the nature of their venom, they are considered to be the most dangerous family of poisonous snakes. About 270 different species make up the elapids, which occur mainly in tropical and subtropical regions of North and South America, Asia, Africa and Australia, while the seasnakes range from the coasts of East Africa to Asia, and from tropical America to Australia. Some elapids are cryptically-coloured to blend in with their surroundings, but many others are ringed with bright, contrasting warning colours, signalling beyond any possible doubt their deadly nature to would-be assailants.

The family Elapidae is often divided into two groups: the cobras and closely-related snakes such as the mambas, the kraits and the coral snakes, and the seasnakes. The cobras and their allies are essentially land-based, inhabiting a wide range of locations including forest, grassland, scrub and desert. Most are terrestrial but some climb trees, enter the water or even burrow under the ground. Perhaps one of the most enduring and powerful images relating to snakes is that of an aggressive cobra, rearing up with its

'hood' extended, a display which is no idle boast. When threatened or disturbed, cobras rise up and spread their long neck ribs to produce the characteristic flaps of skin on either side of the head and neck. This makes them appear even larger and therefore more threatening to a potential enemy. The king cobra (*Ophiophagus hannah*) is the world's largest venomous snake and contains enough venom to kill an elephant, but other cobras are equally lethal. Each year, cobras and kraits cause the deaths of thousands of human beings in India and other parts of Asia. The spitting cobras (*Naja* species) have special fangs through which they can violently force

FAR LEFT
An arboreal snake photographed in the Berenty Reserve, Madagascar.

BELOW
*A false coral snake (*Pliocercus euryzonus*) found in Costa Rica.*

*The cape cobra (*Naja nivea*) feeds on rodents, birds, other snakes and lizards, killing its prey with its highly neurotoxic venom. It is diurnal and occurs in South Africa, where it inhabits rodent burrows, disused termite mounds and rock crevices.*

or spit venom. The spitting cobra can accurately spit its toxic venom into the eyes of an enemy from several feet away while it makes its own escape. Human beings who have been unlucky enough to feel the effect of the venom say it causes excruciating pain and

unless the venom is washed out quickly can cause permanent blindness. The spitting cobra (*Naja nigricollis*) is found in Africa, but the Indian cobra (*Naja naja*) of Asia can also spit venom into its enemy's eyes.

The Indian cobra is one of the cobras

frequently used by so-called snake charmers. Kept securely in a lidded basket until required to perform, it is suddenly thrust into the 'limelight' when the lid is removed. Feeling threatened, the cobra rears up out of the basket, hood extended, while keeping its gaze

focused on the end of the snake charmer's seemingly threatening flute. As the snake charmer waves the flute, so the cobra moves its head to maintain its focus, giving the impression that it is 'dancing' to the sound of the flute, even though the sounds made by it are beyond the snake's range of hearing.

Cobra venom is also used, of course, to paralyse or kill prey prior to swallowing it. The Indian cobra uses its venom to overpower frogs, lizards and rodents, but the scientific name of the king cobra – *Ophiophagus* – gives a clue to its food preferences. The word means 'snake-eater', and snakes do indeed form the bulk of the king cobra's diet, although it also eats large lizards such as monitors. Despite the reputation of venomous

FAR LEFT

A highly venomous Indian cobra (Naja naja), with hood extended. When threatened, it assumes this characteristic pose, where it elongates its long, flexible neck ribs and loose skin to form the distinctive hood. It forces venom through its fangs by exerting muscular pressure on its poison glands, causing jets of venom to be ejected.

LEFT

A snake charmer with cobras and a python in Sri Lanka.

*An Indian cobra (*Naja naja*) rearing up with hood inflated.*

snakes to despatch all kinds of mammals, there is one that is more than a match for snakes such as kraits and cobras. This is the mongoose, a small, rat-like creature related to the civets and genets; in any encounter between a cobra and a mongoose, it is the mongoose that will normally be the winner. The mongoose is an extremely agile, fast-moving creature, easily able to avoid the venomous lunges of the snake. It also has stiff fur that helps to protect it from the cobra's teeth. Armed with razor-sharp teeth of its own, the mongoose darts about, keeping well out of range and waiting for an opening. Suddenly, it gets its chance, seizing the cobra by the back of the neck, and kills it. The mongoose was immortalized in 1894 by the author Rudyard Kipling in *The Jungle Book*, when he described how Rikki-Tikki-Tavi protected a British family living in India from dangerous snakes.

The mambas are highly venomous, fast-moving, slender-bodied snakes found in Africa, which spend most of their time in trees and feed on lizards and birds, while the eastern green mamba (*Dendroaspis angusticeps*) lives in trees on the African savanna. In the mating season, males compete in fighting rituals for the females, entwining their bodies and threatening one another with raised heads in a mating process that in itself may last for several hours. The female lays up to 15 eggs in a hole in the ground or a tree hollow, which hatch after 18 weeks. The slender black mamba (*Dendroaspis polylepis*) is perhaps the fastest land snake and can attain speeds of up to 12mph (19km/h) in short bursts over level

*The black mamba (*Dendroapsis polylepis*) is highly poisonous. It occurs in East Africa from south of Ethiopia down to the south-west of the continent. It feeds on small mammals and birds, which it kills by paralysing them. It gets its name from the colour of the lining of its mouth, which it displays when threatened.*

RIGHT and OPPOSITE
The bright markings of the coral
*snake (*Micrurus nigrocinctus*) are a*
highly visible warning that it is
extremely poisonous.

ground. It is responsible for many human fatalities each year.

The coral snakes live in Asia and the Americas. Not especially aggressive but still highly poisonous, they have short fangs and may need to bite several times to ensure the desired result from their venom. The eastern coral snake (*Micrurus fulvius*) of the U.S.A. and Mexico grows to about 4ft (1.2m) in length. Its body is brightly marked with bands of black, yellow and red that serve as a warning to other predators that it is highly venomous. The eastern coral snake is often mimicked by species such as the similarly marked but harmless scarlet kingsnake (*Lampropeltis triangulum*), but the sequence of the coloured bands on their bodies tells them apart. In the scarlet kingsnake, the yellow bands are separated from the red by bands of black, whereas in the eastern coral snake the yellow bands butt directly up to the red bands. People who are likely to encounter these snakes often remind themselves which one is dangerous by repeating the saying

OPPOSITE
*An olive seasnake (*Aipysurus laevis*) on the seabed, Great Barrier Reef, Australia.*

LEFT
*The yellow-lipped seakrait (*Laticauda colubrina*) produces a highly poisonous venom with a very strong neurotoxin.*

This yellow-lipped seakrait belongs to a species that often comes ashore – many others do not.

'Red on yellow – kill a fellow'.

The elapids are most abundant in Australia where over three-quarters of all snakes are of a highly venomous nature. The largest of the poisonous elapids is the 12-ft (3.7-m) long taipan (*Oxyuranus scutellatus*), also found in New Guinea. Deciding which of these snakes is the most venomous is a more difficult matter, however. The taipan's venom can kill a human being in minutes, yet the seasnake *Hydrophis belcherii* has a venom a hundred times more toxic. The most venomous land snake is probably the 6-ft (1.8-m) long smooth-scaled snake (*Parademansia microlepidotus*) of Queensland and New South Wales, which carries enough venom to kill 125,000 mice. Other highly venomous species include the tiger snake (*Notechis scutatus*) of South Australia and Tasmania and the 5-ft (1.5-m) long eastern brown snake (*Pseudonaja textilis*).

The seasnakes are thought to have evolved from cobras – all highly adapted for a life spent in the oceans. The seakraits (*Laticauda* species) come ashore to breed and lay their eggs, but many other species never leave the water, giving birth to their live young at sea. All seasnakes are highly venomous creatures armed with fast-acting poisons, a necessity if the prey is not to escape into the ocean depths after it has been bitten. Food is almost exclusively fish and their eggs, though some species of seasnakes are highly selective in the prey they prefer. Although they are seldom seen in the wild by human beings, some seasnakes are extremely common; it is estimated that the widespread yellow-bellied seasnake (*Pelamis platurus*) is

the most abundant reptile on earth.

The banded seasnake (*Hydrophis cyanocinctus*) is found in the Persian Gulf, the Indian and the Pacific Oceans, and displays many of the typical features of its type. About 6.5ft (2m) in length, it has a thick body and a small head, with a tail that is laterally flattened to form a paddle-like swimming aid. It breathes air like all other snakes, but can dive for up to two hours at a time. As it does so, pads of tissue block off the nostrils to prevent water from entering the lungs. Like many others of its kind, the muscles of the banded seasnake have degenerated as a result of living constantly in the sea, making it virtually helpless if washed ashore.

Conservation status: seven species are classed as Vulnerable.

FAMILY VIPERIDAE

The family Viperidae, the vipers, is the last of the three families that go to make up the group of advanced snakes and includes about 230 species. In a few systems of classification, the pit vipers are split off into a separate family, the Crotalinae, but here we are including them within the family Viperidae. The Viperidae have a wide global distribution, being found from Canada south to Argentina. They are also distributed throughout all of Africa, except Madagascar, and east to west across all of Eurasia from southern Siberia down to the East Indies.

Vipers are heavy-bodied snakes, characterized by their possession of a single pair of long, hollow fangs situated on the maxilla bones in the upper jaw. Normally

concealed in fleshy tissue, the fangs are swung forward when they are to be used for biting, and deliver their venom from glands on either side of the reptile's head. The glands are large, as are the muscles that contract to pump the venom from the glands, and these result in the viper's characteristically broad, triangular-shaped head. The eyes of vipers have vertical, elliptically-shaped pupils. Most vipers live and hunt on the ground, but a few take to the trees and many are good swimmers. The ground-dwelling species, in particular, need to blend in with vegetation on the forest floor or in scrub and desert-like habitats, which is why so many of them have typically cryptically-patterned skins with dark-red, brown or black markings on a lighter background. Most species of vipers give birth to live young.

Food usually consists of frogs, lizards, birds and mammals. In a typical viper strike, the snake lies in wait to ambush its prey or, guided by scent or the victim's body-heat, approaches the victim unseen. When in range, it coils, then lunges forward at great speed, and with mouth wide open and fangs swung down ready for action, injects a lethal dose of venom into the prey. As the prey writhes in its death throes, the viper retreats a safe distance and waits for the poison to take effect. Only when the prey is dead does the viper approach and proceed to devour its meal. So sensitive are the sensory systems of some species, especially the pit vipers, that all this deadly activity may take place in conditions of total darkness, without the snake ever actually seeing its victim. If there is any possibility of the prey, for example a

RIGHT
*Wagler's pit viper (*Trimeresurus
wagleri*). See also page 258.*

OPPOSITE
*Adders or vipers (*Vipera berus*) are
widely distributed throughout
Eurasia.*

bird, getting away when the snake is attacking it, the snake usually maintains its bite until the prey is dead.

The Gaboon viper (*Bitis gabonica*) is a large snake (up to about 6ft/1.8m in length) that inhabits rainforest in Africa. Its

cryptically-coloured skin patterning helps it to remain concealed on the forest floor by day, and at night it hunts for frogs, toads, rodents and ground birds. It has the longest fangs of any viper, measuring up to almost 2in (5cm) in length in large specimens.

The rare desert sidewinding viper (*Vipera peringueyi*) of the coastal sand dunes of the Namibian desert gets its name from its curious way of moving along in the hot, loose sand. Instead of crawling along the ground in the manner of most other snakes,

OPPOSITE
*This puff adder (*Bitis arietans*) is swimming and showing its chevron-shaped black bars to advantage. This is a viviparous species and large litters, usually comprising 20–40 young, are born in late summer. However, very large females in East Africa have had as many as 156.*

LEFT
*A puff adder with a male leucadendron (*Leucadendron arcuatum*). The puff adder is a short stubby snake with a triangular head distinct from the rest of its body. It is bad-tempered and is quick to strike any intruder with its strongly haemotoxic venom.*

RIGHT

RIGHT
*An emerald pit viper (*Bothriopsis
bilineata*) eating a mouse.*

OPPOSITE
*These bushmasters (*Lachesis muta*),*
the largest of the family containing
the pit vipers, are very well
camouflaged on this rainforest floor
in Costa Rica.

the viper uses the special sidewinding motion
adopted by many snakes that live in hot,
sandy deserts (see page 262 – Legless
Locomotion). To avoid the heat of the day, the
snake buries itself in the sand, which it can do
in under half a minute.

The puff adder (*Bitis arietans*) is another
African species of viper, with a range that
extends into the Middle East. This snake is
found on savanna and is perhaps the most
common in Africa, getting its name from its
habit of hissing and puffing up its body to
make itself look larger than it is when
threatened. The puff adder has 0.5-in (1.3-cm)
long fangs which inject venom causing
haemorrhaging in the victim. Although mainly
a ground-dwelling species, the puff adder
sometimes climbs trees and also swims. It
will eat most vertebrate animals small enough
to swallow, including frogs, lizards, toads,
birds, rats and mice. The female puff adder
produces up to 40 eggs which remain inside
her body until they have developed, and
which hatch shortly after being laid.

Europe's most widespread example is
probably the common viper or adder (*Vipera
berus*). It frequents moorland, fields and
forest margins, seeking out frogs, lizards,
small mammals such as mice and voles, and
birds' eggs. A mainly ground-dwelling
species, nevertheless the common viper does
sometimes enter water in search of prey and
swims well. The common viper is about 20-in
(51-cm) long and, like others of its family, has
powerful venom. It is the only poisonous
snake found in Britain, where it has
occasionally caused death to human beings.
Like many other venomous snakes, the

RIGHT and OPPOSITE RIGHT
The North African desert horned
*viper (*Cerastes cerastes*) lives in*
deserts in north Africa, Israel and
Arabia. It can burrow rapidly into
the sand so that only the two horns
above the eyes are visible above the
surface. Beneath the sand, it will
ambush any prey that ventures too
near.

OPPOSITE LEFT
*The eyelash viper (*Bothrops*
schegelii), from Central America,
has a cluster of spine-like scales
over each eye.

newly-hatched young of the common adder come fully equipped with venom and fangs and are very quickly able to despatch their own prey.

Much more dangerous to human beings is the saw-scaled viper (*Echis carinatus*), its common name arising from the saw-edged scales on the sides of its body. When threatened, it coils its body tightly so that it can rub the scales together, making a loud rasping sound to deter enemies. The saw-scaled viper hides by day under large rocks or dead tree trunks, or may dig itself into the sand of its arid habitat, emerging at night to feed on lizards, small rodents and invertebrates such as centipedes and scorpions. Breeding usually occurs during the rainy season. It can be found from the

northern part of Africa through the Middle East to India, and is to blame for many of the human deaths from snake bites that occur in North Africa; it may even be responsible for more human deaths than any other species throughout the world.

The pit vipers get their name from the sensory pits located in front of and below the eyes on either side of the head. The pits detect the heat given out by warm-blooded prey and help these nocturnal snakes to steer unerringly towards their target. The pit vipers are represented in eastern Europe and are also found in Asia, but the best-known members of the family are probably the various species found in the Americas, particularly the rattlesnakes of southern Canada, the U.S.A. and Mexico. Rattlesnakes

RIGHT
A coiled canebrake rattlesnake
*(*Crotalus horridus atricaudatus*).*
This occurs in lowland areas such as
swamps, canebrakes and riverine
thickets.

OPPOSITE
*The head of the Gaboon viper (*Bitis
gabonica*), showing disruptive*
coloration.

have tail rattles that give the group their name, and are composed of a series of flat, interlocking horny segments that produce the characteristic, sizzling noise when the tail is shaken as a warning by a disturbed rattlesnake. Each time the snake sheds its skin, a new segment is added to the rattle, although some break off with age. A Western movie would hardly be complete without a 'rattler' making its appearance on the prairie –

coiled, but with its head raised and tail erect and producing that familiar sound.

The largest rattlesnake is the eastern diamondback (*Crotalus adamanteus*). Found across farmland and woodland in the eastern U.S.A., it is also considered to be the most dangerous snake in North America. The warning from its rattle is not to be taken lightly, for rattlesnake venom is highly potent and a bite from this species is enough

to kill a man within an hour. The eastern diamondback rattlesnake is clearly identifiable by the conspicuous diamond patterning on its skin that serves to camouflage it as it lies coiled among low vegetation, ready to ambush birds and rabbits. The western diamondback rattlesnake (*Crotalus atrox*) has a similar pattern of diamond markings on its skin, is about 7-ft (2.1-m) long, and is found on the western side of the U.S.A., in Arkansas,

RIGHT
*Black-tailed rattlesnake (*Crotalus
molossus*). A typical pit viper, the
heat-sensitive pits can be seen just
below and in front of the eyes.*

OPPOSITE
*A western diamondback rattlesnake
(*Crotalus atrox*) showing
threatening behaviour.*

Texas, Oklahoma, southern New Mexico,
Arizona and California and on into Mexico. It
prefers dry habitats such as desert flats and
rocky hillsides, but can also be found by
rivers and along coastal prairies. Like its
relative, the eastern diamondback, the
western diamondback is another large and
dangerous species.

Another highly venomous American
snake, the cottonmouth or water moccasin
(*Agkistrodon piscivorus*) is a dark-coloured,
heavy-bodied reptile that spends much of its
life in swamps, rivers and lakes in the south
and eastern U.S.A. The cottonmouth can grow
to about 6ft (1.8-m) in length, although
smaller individuals are often encountered.
It is predominantly nocturnal, slipping
quietly into the water at nightfall to prey on
fish and amphibians, although it also eats birds
and is one of very few species of snakes to
consume carrion. Its venom is primarily
haemotoxic; a bite from the cottonmouth
causes the destruction of the red blood cells
and other tissues and prevents blood from
coagulating. The female cottonmouth produces
up to 15 young.

A close relative of the cottonmouth, the
3-ft (0.9-m) long copperhead or highland
moccasin (*Agkistrodon contortrix*) is the most
common venomous snake in the eastern
U.S.A. However, the venom of the
copperhead is less toxic than the cottonmouth
and causes few fatalities in human beings,
which is just as well, since it bites more
people than any other snake in North
America. Young copperheads have a yellow
tip to the end of their tails which they wave
enticingly to encourage small creatures, such

RIGHT and OPPOSITE
The sidewinder (Crotalus cerastes) is
perfectly adapted to desert
conditions. The curious pattern left
in the sand is caused by the
sidewinder's method of locomotion,
which is designed to avoid body
contact with hot sand for any length
of time.

as frogs, to come within range of their fangs.
This way of attracting prey is highly useful
for the snake because it saves energy that
would otherwise be spent actively hunting. It
also enables it to keep a lower profile and
thus limit its own exposure to predators.

The fer-de-lance (*Bothrops atrox*) is a
large pit viper found from Mexico to South
America and in the West Indies, where it
inhabits coastal regions. The manushi or
Asiatic pit viper (*Agkistrodon halys*) is found
from the region of the Caspian Sea to China.
This is one of only a few pit vipers in the Old
World, where it hibernates through the winter.
Its venom is fatal to small animals like
rodents but usually only causes temporary
paralysis in human victims. Much more
deadly is the bushmaster (*Lachesis muta*), the
longest of all vipers at between 8–11.5ft
(2.4–3.5m) in length and the only New World
viper to lay eggs. It is found from Central
America as far down as the Amazon basin in
South America. A nocturnal snake, hiding by
day in tree hollows or other secluded places,
the bushmaster preys on various kinds of
mammals up to the size of small deer.

Conservation status: seven species are
Critically Endangered; four species are
Endangered; seven species are Vulnerable.

CHAPTER SIX
TUATARA

RIGHT and OPPOSITE
The Cook Strait tuatara (Sphenodon
punctatus) *is a living fossil reptile,*
found on Takapourewa (Stephens
Island) in the Cook Strait, New
Zealand. The two species of New
Zealand tuatara are the only
surviving members of the reptile
order Rhynchcephalia, which was
present during the dinosaur age.

The tuatara is the sole living representative
not only of a family (Sphenodontidae)
but also of a complete order, the
Rhynchocephalia, all other members of the
order being long since extinct and known only
from fossils. The Rhynchocephalia appeared
some 220 million years ago during the
Mesozoic period, before the first dinosaurs
roamed the Earth. The order was once
distributed throughout parts of Europe, Africa,
North and South America and Asia, but by the
end of the Mesozoic period, about 65 million
years ago, all members had died out – except
for the tuatara. Fossil evidence tells us that the
living tuatara closely resembles examples of
the species that existed over 150 million years
ago, which allows us a rare insight into the
biology and behaviour of prehistoric species.

The tuatara is a solid-looking reptile
which grows to about 25in (64cm) in length,
although females are somewhat smaller. The
head is large when compared with the rest of
the body, with a large mouth and large eyes.
A whitish crest runs from the rear of the head
down the back and tail. The word tuatara
means 'peaks on the back' in the Maori

RIGHT
Replica of a fossil of Homoesaurus
maximiliani *(formerly* Kallimodon*),
a sphenodont lizard that lived on
land. It is a fossil relative of the
living fossil tuatara,* Sphenodon
punctatus, *found in New Zealand
today.*

FAR RIGHT
*Detail of the head of a Cook Strait
tuatara.*

OPPOSITE
*Marlborough Sound, seen from the
summit of Takapourewa in the Cook
Strait between the North and South
islands of New Zealand. This island
is the only place where the
endangered* Sphenodon punctatus *is
to be found.*

language, and refers to this crest, which is
more prominent in males and can be raised as
a threat display. The body is variously
coloured grey, olive-green or tinged pinkish,
with speckles of white or grey with a paler
underside. Forgetting for a moment that this
is a relatively small creature, one could easily
imagine the tuatara, basking on a rock with
its crest of spines erect, a prehistoric monster
in miniature.

Until quite recently, it was thought that
there was only one species of tuatara, but in
1989 scientists working at Victoria University
in Wellington, New Zealand, discovered that

there were in fact two distinct species. (This
discovery was made using DNA analysis, a
method which has caused scientists to rethink
the classification and naming of many plants
and animals.) The most common species is
Sphenodon punctatus, sometimes called the
Cook Strait tuatara. There is also a
subspecies of *Sphenodon punctatus* called the
northern tuatara. The other species is the
much rarer, and slightly smaller, Brother's
Island or Gunther's tuatara (*Sphenodon
guntheri*).

A Reptile Apart
Apart from its unusual classificatory position,

the tuatara is unique in other ways. It looks
rather like a lizard, and when first discovered
it was originally thought to be a kind of
lizard. Indeed, it is sometimes still called the
'tuatara lizard'. However, a curator at the
British Museum in the 1860s examined a
preserved specimen and discovered that it
bore a number of features that were unique
and that clearly separate it from the true
lizards of the order Squamata, namely that
the vertebrae have hollow ends and the skull
has two bony arches like that of a
crocodilian, when in lizards one or both
arches are usually missing. The word
Sphenodontidae means wedge-toothed, and

FAR RIGHT
*Detail of the crest of the Cook Strait
tuatara.*

BELOW
*Tuatara skull showing large orbital
socket, teeth fixed to the edges of the
jaws and the horny beak on the
upper jaw.*

BELOW RIGHT
Cast skin of a Cook Strait tuatara.

refers to the fact that the sharp, saw-like teeth
are fused with the jaw bones instead of being
separate structures. Male tuataras lack a
penis, and all tuataras are without visible ear
openings and middle ears. The tuatara's heart
is the most primitive type found in living
reptiles, and some aspects of its brain
anatomy are also quite primitive. Like
lizards, however, a tuatara can regenerate its
tail if it loses it and, like most other reptiles,
shed its skin annually to allow for growth.

The tuatara is active from dusk to dawn,
and requires the lowest temperature of any
living reptile. Temperatures as low as 53° F
(12° C) suit it quite well, and it can even
tolerate temperatures as low as 41° F (5° C),
whereas most other reptiles prefer
temperatures of 77° F (25° C) or even more.
Nevertheless, the tuatara still likes to bask in

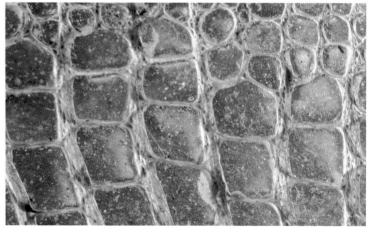

TUATARA

A Cook Strait tuatara emerging from its burrow.

the sun like other reptiles to warm itself up. Because of its tolerance of low temperatures, the tuatara is able to survive in regions that other reptiles would find too cold, which explains why it has managed to maintain a foothold on a few rocky islands in the cool latitudes off the coast of New Zealand. It is not found anywhere else. The nocturnal

lifestyle of the tuatara has resulted in some other special adaptations: the retina, the light-reflecting layer found in the eyes of vertebrates, has special cells that allow the tuatara to see well when light levels are low as well as in strong sunlight. The metabolism and growth rate of the reptile are also slow; it can take 20 years for a tuatara to reach sexual

maturity, and individuals may live for over 100 years, continuing to grow until they are 50 or 60 years old.

Another unusual feature is that the pineal body, a part of the tuatara's brain, is connected to a 'third eye' located in the top of the head. Although the third eye, or parietal, has many of the features of an eye, such as a

OPPOSITE
A tuatara with a regenerated tail.

LEFT
A tuatara in a tree at night.

The habitat of the tuatara is in holes burrowed into the surface of Takapourewa.

TUATARA

ABOVE and ABOVE RIGHT
Eye of the tuatara showing the pupil
tightly closed by day and wide open
at night.

lens and a retina, it cannot form images and is not sensitive to light. It is thought that it absorbs the sun's ultra-violet rays in the first few months of its life, enriching the body with vitamin D and helping the animal to develop properly. From about four to six months of age, the third eye is gradually covered over with scales.

Life On the Rocks
Millions of years ago, the Earth's continents were much closer together than they are now, and land animals could roam across vast landscapes more or less at will, provided they encountered the conditions that suited them. As the continents slowly moved apart and into smaller land masses, however, the seas and oceans that formed between them made effective barriers to the passage of most land-based creatures. When New Zealand became separated, about 80 million years ago, its animal life became isolated – exactly the same fate that befell many other island fauna separated by extensive stretches of water. Significantly, many of the highly efficient mammalian land predators had not yet evolved at the time of the separation, and so never reached New Zealand. The region's animal life – that includes the flightless kiwi and large, curious ground-dwelling parrots, as well as species like the tuatara – was therefore able to live free from the competition and predation that caused the demise of many other ancient animal lineages. Consequently, while its close relatives were facing extinction through predation and competition in most other parts of the world, the tuatara continued to flourish.

About 1,000 years ago, the tuatara was more widely spread throughout New Zealand, but the advent of human beings brought livestock, dogs, rats and other introduced animals that quickly caused the decimation of the reptile on the mainland. Some say that the tuatara was extinct on the mainland even before the arrival of European settlers, but it had certainly disappeared by the late 1800s. The tuatara is now found on about 30 inaccessible, steep, rocky islands dotted around the coast of New Zealand, where invasions by other animals were limited both by the terrain and the unpredictable seas. About 60,000 tuataras live on Stephen's Island in the Marlborough Sound, and others live on the Trios group of islands, also in the Marlborough Sound. The subspecies *Sphenodon punctatus punctatus* lives on Little Barrier Island and on

FAR LEFT
Cook Strait tuatara.

BELOW
Tick specific to the Cook Strait tuatara.

OPPOSITE
Stephens Island, showing grazed and ungrazed land separated by a fence.

LEFT
A Cook Strait tuatara emerging from a burrow it shares with fairy prions.

TUATARA

about 24 others, while the Brother's Island tuatara lives on North Brother Island in the Marlborough Sound. There are only about 400 adults of this species alive in the wild, consequently their existence is precarious. Some tuataras now live once more on the mainland, but this time in protected reserves such as the one at Invercargill Museum.

Tuataras are ground-living reptiles and spend much of their time sheltering in burrows, some of which they dig themselves in loose soil; but they often occupy those excavated by burrow-nesting seabirds such as shearwaters and prions. Tuataras sometimes abuse their avian hosts' hospitality by eating chicks or eggs, but by the same token, young tuataras sometimes fall victim to hungry seabirds. The tuatara's chief diet, however, consists of insects such as beetles and crickets, worms, snails, eggs, small lizards and even young tuataras. Food is mostly caught on nocturnal forays, although young

tuataras often feed during the day to avoid encountering hungry adults at night.

Tuataras are sexually mature when they are about 15–20 years old, with females breeding every two to five years on average. Mating takes place in the southern hemisphere's spring and summer. The method of mating is different from that of lizards, in that the male tuatara does not have a penis; he simply mounts the female and passes sperm

348

TUATARA

OPPOSITE LEFT
Cook Strait tuatara.

OPPOSITE ABOVE RIGHT
A tuatara featured on a New Zealand postage stamp.

OPPOSITE BELOW RIGHT
A weta (Hemiandra sp.), a grasshopper-like insect with outsized antennae found only in New Zealand, and which is eaten by tuataras.

LEFT
A female tuatara watching the approach of a male from her position up a tree.

from his cloaca into hers. The pregnant female excavates a burrow about 4-in (10-cm) deep, into which she deposits up to 10 leathery eggs. The incubation period is the longest of any reptile, being between 12 to 16 months. Scientists investigating the breeding habits of captive tuataras have discovered that the temperature at which the eggs are incubated determines the sex of the young hatchlings. They found that at 64° F (18° C) all hatchlings were female, while at 68° F (20° C) about 80 per cent developed into females. At 70° F (21° C) about half were female and half were male, but at 71.5° F (22° C) 80 per cent were likely to be male.

In the wild, there is no parental involvement with either the eggs or the young, and once the baby tuatara has released itself by

TUATARA

slitting open the shell with its egg tooth, it must fend for itself. At birth, tuataras are just over 2in (5cm) in length, and usually hide under rocks and logs or dig themselves burrows to avoid being eaten at this vulnerable stage of their existence.

Most of the remaining tuatara populations are now fairly secure, due largely to recovery programmes designed to maintain and increase populations, as well as rigid conservation laws. The general remoteness of their island refuges, kept free from predators such as Polynesian rats, has also been a major factor in ensuring these survivors of a bygone age remain to this day.

Conservation status: *Sphenodon guntheri* is classed as Vulnerable

CHAPTER SEVEN
CROCODILIANS

The crocodilians comprise the order
Crocodylia. The word crocodilian is used as
a collective description of the main groups of
reptiles in the order, namely the alligators, the
crocodiles and the gharial. Together with the
birds, crocodilians are the only survivors of the
once-dominant Archosauria, which was a group
of diapsid reptiles (reptiles with two holes, or
aspses, in the temporal region of their skulls) that
included the mighty dinosaurs as well as many
other kinds of reptiles, such as the flying
pterosaurs. At their peak, the archosaurs – or
ruling reptiles as they are known – dominated all
life on land and in the oceans. Most crocodilians
had evolved by the late Triassic period, about 200
million years ago, and those alive today have
changed little in the last 65 million years or so.
However, this should not be taken as an indication
that existing crocodilians are mere relics of a
bygone glorious age, teetering on the very edge of
extinction – far from it: crocodilians are among
the most advanced of all the reptiles – in some
aspects *the* most advanced – and are supreme
masters of their environment. There are 23
living species of crocodilians.

As a group, crocodilians range across

CROCODILIANS

south-eastern U.S.A., down into South America and over many parts of Africa, southern Asia, China, the East and West Indies and Australia. Most of them live in the tropics, but two species are found outside. These are the American alligator (*Alligator mississippiensis*) of the south-eastern U.S.A. and the Chinese alligator (*Alligator sinensis*) of the Yangtse river region. Crocodilians are not generally found in climates colder than temperate regions, nor are they found at any significant elevation; they are strictly lowland creatures. Once upon a time some huge crocodilians lived on earth. *Deinosuchus* grew to a length of 49ft (15m) and boasted 6.5-ft (2-m) jaws; in fact, today's biggest crocodilians, although still large, would be dwarfed by such a creature. The biggest species alive is the saltwater or estuarine crocodile (*Crocodylus porosus*) at 23ft (7m) in length, while the dwarf crocodile (*Osteolaemus tetraspis*) of the upper Congo river in West Africa is probably the smallest species at only 5ft (1.5m) in length. Male crocodilians are larger than females, but apart from size differences there are no other features that readily separate the sexes of

most species. The exception is the gharial (*Gavialis gangeticus*), the males having a bulbous structure at the end of their noses. Many crocodilians are long-lived, with some species surviving for 60 years or more in the wild, and even longer in captivity.

The skin of a crocodilian is made up of non-overlapping scales and is frequently studded with bony plates called scutes. When a crocodilian sheds its skin, it does so by losing its scales individually, instead of all at once like snakes or in large pieces like lizards. Internally, crocodilians have several important differences when compared with other reptiles. First, the brain has a fully developed cerebral cortex (the part responsible for intelligence in animals such as mammals).

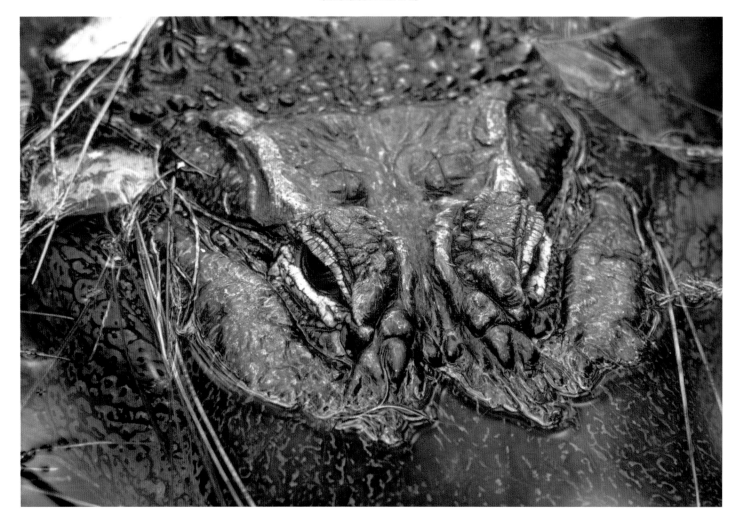

Because of this, crocodilians are capable of learning new types of behaviour instead of continuing to act instinctively. The design of the crocodilian heart is also more advanced than that of other reptiles, in the majority of which the two sides of the ventricle (one of the heart's chambers) are not separated, which means there is some mixing of oxygenated and unoxygenated blood. In crocodilians, the ventricles are almost completely separated by a wall of tissue, helping to maintain a better oxygenated blood supply to vital organs such as the brain.

Water Specialists

Of all living reptiles, none conjures up an image of archaic, lumbering, almost dinosaur-like menace quite as perfectly as a crocodilian. Armoured, scaly, often huge and powerful, and armed with terrifying jaws and teeth, most crocodilians are every bit as dangerous as they look. All of them are carnivores, feeding on a wide range of animal prey which occasionally includes human beings. There is no mistaking any member of the order, for the shape of all crocodilians is essentially similar: a long-snouted head carried horizontally in front of an elongated body, four legs projecting from the sides but capable of lifting the body well clear of the

OPPOSITE
Detail of the eyes of an American alligator.

LEFT
Detail of the scaly skin and the claws of the front foot of a Nile crocodile.

OPPOSITE
A spectacled caiman (Caiman crocodilus) in Venezuela. Crocodilians are highly effective on land, despite their aquatic lifestyles.

LEFT
Saltwater (saltie) or estuarine crocodile (Crocodylus porosus). Kakadu National Park, Australia.

CROCODILIANS

ground, and a long, flattened, muscular tail.

The similar lifestyles exhibited by most species mean that other details of their anatomy are also duplicated. Because all crocodilians are aquatic or amphibious creatures, the crescent-shaped nostrils are set high on the top of the nose tip, enabling them to breathe even when lying almost submerged in the water. The eyes are similarly placed high on the head to allow for optimum vision when in this position. They are also set fairly close together to facilitate binocular vision – an important consideration for an animal that relies on accurate perception of depth when snatching its prey. Crocodilians have vertical,

cat-like pupils that dilate to enable them to see well in low light conditions, although they do not see especially well under water. A mirror-like layer of cells at the back of the eye also helps to improve their night vision. The nostrils and the ears are closed by flaps when the reptile submerges, preventing water from entering. At the same time, the eyes are protected by a transparent third eyelid, or nictitating membrane. At the back of the mouth there is a flap of skin called a false palate that closes over the windpipe to enable it to feed when submerged without swallowing water at the same time and thus drowning.

Crocodilians do not hibernate, though

they may sink to the bottom of rivers or lakes where it is slightly warmer to sleep when the temperature drops. Their metabolism slows during sleep, and they can normally get by without needing to surface to breathe fresh air. If oxygen supplies to the vital organs become too low, however, they move up to the surface again to breathe in more air.

The front feet of crocodilians have five separate toes, but the back feet have four, which are partly webbed. On land, crocodilians walk with their bodies raised off the ground; their ankles swivel so that their legs are almost underneath the body. When moving like this, the gait resembles that of a

American alligator (Alligator mississippiensis), hauled out on a grassy knoll in the Okefenokee swamp, Georgia, U.S.A.

mammal and is considered to be a more advanced method of walking than the one adopted by lizards. Crocodilians can move quite fast when required: a galloping motion, during which the reptile seems to be bouncing along, is sometimes used, and speeds of up to 10mph (16km/h) have been observed. Sometimes crocodilians adopt a more lizard-like method of walking, moving one foot at a time while the belly scrapes along the ground. A crocodilian's willingness to move over land varies according to the species: estuarine crocodiles seldom venture more than a body's length from the water's edge, whereas the mugger (*Crocodylus palustris*) may travel long distances over land, especially if it needs to find alternative sources of water, for example, when there is drought. The dwarf crocodile (*Osteolaemus tetraspis*) lives in streams in West African tropical forests but unusually also makes long night-time excursions inland to look for food.

But it is in water that crocodilians find their true element. Although the back feet are webbed, it is the tail that provides the main propulsion. When swimming, the huge, muscular tail is lashed from side to side in an S-shaped motion, with the legs often held against the body to help reduce drag. Speeds of up to 12mph (20km/h) can be achieved using this method – about as fast as a powerboat. But the webbed feet do have their uses in the water: by using an upward movement of the feet a crocodilian can rapidly sink backwards and downwards if threatened. It is also possible for it to float high in the water by inflating its lungs or to sink lower by expelling air until only its nose

*Yacarés (*Caiman yacare*), hauled out beside a pool in the dry season in Pantanal, Brazil.*

tip and eyes are visible.

Although all crocodilians are highly aquatic, most are strictly freshwater species, whose distribution is limited by their intolerance of sea water. There are some exceptions, however. The American crocodile (*Crocodylus acutus*) is an estuarine species that can tolerate salt water, as a result of which its range extends from southern Florida, through Central America, and down as far as northern South America. It is also found on various islands in the Caribbean. The estuarine crocodile (*Crocodylus porosus*) is also known as the saltwater crocodile – a fitting name for a species with a vast range that takes in south-west India, then east to China and south as far as the Philippines, Malaysia, Indonesia, New Guinea and northern Australia.

Crocodilian Behaviour
Usually, crocodilians are solitary creatures, except when seeking out others of their own kind for mating or when abundant food supplies draw individuals together. They communicate with one another by means of sounds, body postures, smells released from scent glands and by touch. Vocal sounds are made by forcing air through the larynx (voice box) in the throat. Young crocodilians call

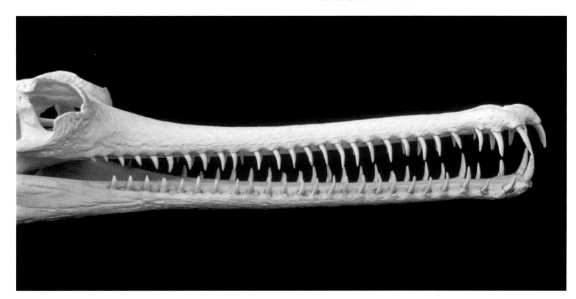

OPPOSITE
A Nile crocodile with jaws closed,
showing its pointed snout. Note the
fourth lower tooth which is visible
when the mouth is closed. This
distinguishes crocodiles from
alligators, in which the tooth is not
visible when the mouth is closed.

LEFT
Replica of the skull of the Ganges
gavial or gharial (Gavialis
gangeticus). *This is a large, rare,*
slender-snouted fish-eating Indian
crocodile. It is considered sacred by
Hindus and is now an endangered
species.

when they are being fed or are in danger, and by calling to one another help to keep the brood together. During mating, a soft purring sound may be emitted, and threatened crocodiles may hiss, growl and grunt. One of the most common sounds, however, is a loud bellow or roar, often repeated. Other, more visual, methods of communication include raising the jaws off the ground while keeping the mouth closed.

Adult crocodilians mark their territories by bringing their heads down heavily onto the water's surface to make a loud slapping sound, or by snapping their jaws together at the surface: such sounds are designed to carry well under water. Dominant individuals often swim higher in the water, while others of the same species may indicate their submission by swimming lower. The dominant animals get the best choice of general habitat, including basking positions, nest sites and food. They also control access to mates at breeding time; in some species territories are only defended during the breeding period. Actual fighting between crocodilians is rare, and most disputes are settled by the various postures and signals described above. If fighting does take place between similar-sized animals competing to be the most dominant, the protagonists usually settle matters by banging the sides of their heads together or engaging in a bout of biting. It is rarely the case that any real damage ensues. If drought conditions prevail, disputes concerning territory are usually temporarily suspended and all the crocodilians cram together in whatever living area is available. On occasions, however, this communal existence reaches breaking point, when in one dry season some 200 alligators were crammed into one resting hole. The problem of overcrowding was reduced, however, when some of the bigger individuals killed the smaller ones!

Like all other reptiles, crocodilians are cold-blooded and must use the temperature of their external surroundings to help regulate their own body temperature. Many species haul themselves out of the water to bask in

OPPOSITE
A Yacaré (Caiman yacare), almost obscured by the vegetation in a Brazilian swamp pool.

LEFT
A Yacaré making a meal of a dead capybara.

CROCODILIANS

FAR RIGHT

A man swimming in a pond built for buddhist monks in Anuradhapura, Sri Lanka. He is hitting the surface of the water to frighten the crocodiles away.

OPPOSITE

*Young Nile crocodiles (*Crocodylus niloticus*) at a crocodile farm in Zimbabwe.*

the sun during the day, especially those living in temperate climates. Large numbers of Yacaré caimans (*Caiman yacare*) still gather en masse to bask on Brazilian riverbanks, where they are an impressive sight; sadly, like other species, their numbers are reduced as they are still being hunted for their skins. If they become too hot they simply slither into the water to cool off. Crocodilians can also cool themselves by opening their mouths and exposing the large, moist surfaces within so that evaporation can take place.

In very hot climates, most species simply stay in the water most of the time. In dry periods, some species wallow in mud so that they are completely coated, which acts as a form of body insulation to protect them from the searing heat of the sun. After they have consumed a large meal, crocodilians usually seek out more heat to help speed up the process of digestion. The cool winters in the Yangtse river region mean that the Chinese alligator (*Alligator sinensis*) must find somewhere warm to survive. It therefore digs itself a burrow in the bank and rest up inside. Sometimes the burrow may have many tunnels and becomes quite an extensive network of underground excavations.

Supreme Hunters

As night falls, a large Nile crocodile (*Crocodylus niloticus*) quietly slips into a waterhole and submerges until just the tip of its nose and its eyes are visible. Floating waterweed coats the top of its body, making it almost impossible to detect. Soon, a small herd of impala comes cautiously to the waterhole to drink. The crocodile glides

smoothly and almost invisibly towards the group and singles out one of them, a juvenile that has waded further into the water than its more cautious relatives. Suddenly, using its strong tail for extra momentum, the crocodile launches itself halfway out of the water, snatches the unfortunate impala in its huge jaws and sinks back into the water with it, scattering the rest of the herd in blind panic. The whole episode is over in a couple of seconds. Now the prey is quickly drowned under water before being ripped apart and swallowed. Such rapid ambushes are typical of the way crocodilians operate. A slightly modified but similar technique enables them even to snatch birds and bats from above the water surface by leaping into the air with a

thrust of their tails. When seen at a zoo or wildlife park, a crocodilian may lie so still that visitors sometimes wonder if it is actually a real specimen at all. Even when floating in the water it often resembles nothing more sinister than a dead log. It is difficult to believe that such a seemingly static creature can explode with such speed and fury when the moment to capture its prey arrives.

Crocodilians are superbly adapted to their chosen method of hunting. Many will attack and eat any kind of animal they can overcome, although some species have distinct preferences and are specially designed to exploit particular food sources. The biggest species have the most varied tastes, the kind of food they prefer changing as they grow.

A child holding a baby crocodile at Crocodile Creek near Ballito, South Africa.

Young individuals will frequently take insects, fish, molluscs and crustaceans, but as they get bigger they tend to go for larger, more sustaining meals such as mammals. To help grip their prey, crocodilians have jaws armed with sharp teeth, those at the front of the mouth being generally slightly curved, while teeth at the back are shorter and more conical. Unlike some other carnivores, the teeth are not designed to slice up food; their job is simply to hold it securely until it can be swallowed whole or torn apart before being gulped down. If a tooth is lost, it is replaced by a new one already lying in place within the pulp cavity of the existing one; an individual may replace 50 or so sets of teeth in its lifetime. Large prey is dismembered by the performance of a twisting or spinning movement in the water that literally tears pieces off the victim's body.

The muscles used to open a crocodilian's mouth are relatively weak; a skilled person can hold the mouth of even a large crocodilian closed with his or her bare hands. But the powerful muscles that close the mouth are another matter altogether. They can close with a force strong enough to crush bone, and are highly effective in preventing the escape of prey once it is caught.

Fish-eating specialists like the gharial (*Gavialis gangeticus*) and the false gharial (*Tomistoma schlegelii*) have long, slender snouts, a shape that offers little resistance in the water, and which helps the reptiles move their heads quickly from side to side to snatch fast-moving fish. They also have up to 100 specialized teeth for grasping slippery prey; when their mouths are held slightly open, their jaws resemble giant zip fasteners. In contrast, caimans, crocodiles and alligators have broader, shorter snouts and can tackle a wider menu, including waterbirds, turtles and a range of mammals, while big species can even overcome large hoofed mammals such as zebra, wildebeest and buffalo. Despite the fact that crocodilians are usually solitaries, abundant food supplies may cause several individuals to come together to feed. Some species have even been seen to hunt cooperatively, then join together to tear large prey apart.

Once swallowed, the prey enters the stomach, where it is partly digested with the aid of strong acids. In fact, the stomach acid of the crocodilian is the strongest recorded for any vertebrate, and helps to break down the bones and shells of its victims. Some species also swallow stones that stay in the stomach to assist the grinding-up process. Up to 60 per cent of digested food may be stored in the form of fat in the crocodilian's body, including the tail. The low metabolism of reptiles, together with such a high-energy form of food storage, mean that large specimens may be able to survive for a year or more without eating.

Throughout history, there have been many instances of human beings being attacked and even eaten by crocodiles and alligators. While we can probably imagine few more horrific ways to lose one's life than to be eaten by a savage wild animal, we should not be unduly surprised that it sometimes happens. To a large hunter, such as a crocodilian, a human being is simply another potential meal. The species most commonly implicated in such

attacks include the wide-ranging estuarine crocodile (*Crocodylus porosus*), the Nile crocodile (*Crocodylus niloticus*) and the American alligator (*Alligator mississippiensis*) – all large, aggressive species which grow to about 17ft (5.2m) or more in length.

There are several other reasons why crocodilians attack human beings, not all to do with predation. Defence of their territory or nest accounts for many instances of attack. Local fishermen, in particular, are at risk

when they stray into areas inhabited by large crocodilians, when they may unwittingly come across the reptile in their search for fish, or may be intending to steal crocodilian eggs or young. Even if the reptile is not defending its territory, it may feel sufficiently threatened by the intrusion to attack. In the wild, most crocodilians are protected species, but they are often reared on special farms because their meat is low in fat and their skins are prized for making items such as shoes and handbags, while many more are kept as tourist

A spectacled caiman baby being handled.

BELOW and OPPOSITE
A warden holding recently hatched
Nile crocodiles.

attractions in zoos and wildlife parks. It is not uncommon for keepers and other handlers to be attacked in such surroundings, but although the victim may be bitten – sometimes quite badly – he or she usually manages to escape.

However, there are plenty of well-documented cases of human beings being completely devoured by crocodiles or alligators. In Africa, the Nile crocodile is responsible for killing or maiming many people each year – probably hundreds –

although accurate statistics are hard to come by. The American alligator is the chief culprit in the U.S.A., though the number is very low, at about four attacks per year; but there are thousands of complaints each year from local residents who have been alarmed to see alligators wandering into built-up areas. The estuarine crocodile is responsible for attacks in places as far apart as India and Australia, while in northern Australia there have been about a dozen deaths attributable to this species since 1982.

In late 2003, a particularly horrific crocodile attack occurred in this region, made all the more shocking because it was witnessed by two survivors of the encounter. During December of that year, three friends, aged between 19 and 22, were riding on quad bikes in the Finniss river area some 60 miles (97km) from Darwin in the Northern Territory. Recent rains had swollen the river to a dangerous level, and one of the riders was swept away by the waters. As his two companions went to his rescue, they saw a large crocodile in the water and, fearing for their lives, fled for safety up a tree. Minutes later the crocodile emerged with the mauled body of their friend in its jaws, almost as if it were showing off its trophy. For the next 22 hours the crocodile stalked the two friends, who were forced to remain in the tree, desperately trying to stay awake for fear of falling into the river. Fortunately, they were eventually winched to safety by a helicopter that had come searching for them. It is thought that an estuarine crocodile, believed to be about 14-ft (4.3-m) long, was responsible for this fatal attack. Such episodes serve to underline the dangers that exist if, by chance, one is unlucky enough to find oneself in a crocodile's territory.

Crocodilian Reproduction
Prior to mating, males perform courtship rituals to attract females. It is common for the male to swim alongside the female and to place his nearest forelimbs and hindlimbs on her body. He may also rub her throat and blow bubbles at her. Following courtship, the pair usually sink to the bottom and copulate,

CROCODILIANS

BELOW
One-year-old spectacled caimans
at a crocodile farm in Venezuela.

OPPOSITE
Young Nile crocodile. Note the
flattened tail for swimming.

the male having a grooved penis that is protruded through a slit in his cloaca. Fertilization takes place internally in all crocodilians, and all species lay eggs. It takes several months following fertilization, however, before the female is ready to lay.

The nest is built at night, on ground above any possible flood level. Some species dig holes in the ground in which to lay their eggs, while others create mounds of vegetation. Hole-diggers include the gharial (*Gavialis gangeticus*), the Nile crocodile

(*Crocodylus niloticus*) and the Australian freshwater crocodile (*Crocodylus johnsoni*). Because the shells have hard, brittle shells like those of birds, the female crocodile is careful to ensure that the eggs do not crack when they are dropped into the hole. Sometimes each egg is laid directly onto one of the female's hindfeet, which is then used to gently lower the egg into the bottom of the hole. After laying her eggs, the female covers the hole with sand, leaving no trace of their presence visible to egg thieves. The gharial

builds its nest close to the bank so that it can be watched constantly without the need for the reptile to leave the water.

Mound nests are a feature of many crocodilian species, and it is among these that the best examples of parental care can also be seen – a rather incongruous activity in such ruthless predators. Estuarine crocodiles (*Crocodylus porosus*), American alligators (*Alligator mississippiensis*) and the spectacled caiman (*Caiman crocodilus*) are among the species that build mounds in which to lay

their eggs. In a quiet area a little distance from the water, the female gathers together grass, leaves, sticks and soil, using her mouth and limbs to form a dome-shaped structure that may be as much as 10-ft (2.5-m) across and 39-in (1-m) high. She then digs a hole in the middle of the mound and lays her eggs in it, about one every minute or so, carefully covering them with more plant debris. The number of eggs laid varies according to the species– the spectacled caiman laying up to about 30 eggs, whereas the estuarine crocodile may lay as many as 90.

As the plant material in the mound slowly rots, the temperature rises to about 88° F (31° C) through bacterial action. This helps to incubate the eggs, during which time they are often carefully guarded by the mother. This is an important safeguard, since the nests, with their rich, protein-filled eggs, are a source of food for raiders such as monkeys, pigs, lizards and even human beings. Estuarine crocodiles (*Crocodylus porosus*) may dig a series of trenches or pits in the vicinity in which to lie up while guarding the nest. At other times they stand guard on top of the mound itself. Other species make regular nocturnal visits to their nests to ensure they are still intact.

All the eggs hatch at the same time, the young hatchlings thrusting the tips of their noses out of their shells, waiting for a sign that the mother is nearby. For example, vibration caused by the mother crawling over the nest will trigger the hatchlings into making high-pitched calls, in response to which the mother will dig open the nest to help the young escape. Any eggs that have not opened will be gently crushed in the

mother's jaws to break the shell and release the hatchling. Now comes perhaps the most touching and unusual display of crocodilian concern. In species such as the Nile and estuarine crocodiles the mother carefully picks up batches of the hatchlings in her jaws, transfers them to a throat pouch, and carries them to the relative safety of the water. Any hatchlings that are not correctly held in the mouth are deftly tossed into the air by the female and caught so that they can be repositioned.

Baby crocodilians may remain with their mothers for several months or even years. Nile crocodiles have special nurseries in quiet waterways where the young can safely grow. In times of danger, the young may hitch a ride on their mother's back, or may even retreat once more to the safety of her mouth while she dives from sight beneath the surface. Young crocodilians are carnivorous from the start of life, and are soon snapping at insects and any other small prey that comes within reach, turning to more substantial items as they grow bigger. Growth is rapid where food is freely available and the temperature remains high all year. Increases of 12in (30cm) are quite common, but a few species can exceed even this. The mugger (*Crocodylus palustris*) of India is about 10in

(25cm) at the time of hatching, but can reach a length of over 3ft (0.9m) by the end of its first year.

As an individual grows, it becomes less likely to fall victim to predation and so its chances of survival increase. Just like many other animals, mortality tends to be highest at the egg and hatchling stages, when the crocodilian is at its smallest and most vulnerable. Eggs do not suffer only at the hands of nest-raiding animals; they may also get washed away if the nest floods due to rising water levels, or they may become overheated during the incubation process, when the developing embryos will die. In some populations of saltwater crocodiles, only about 25 per cent of eggs survive to hatching stage; even in those that do hatch, the chances of the young crocodilian making it to the age of five years is estimated at no more than about 30 to 60 per cent. The enemies of young crocodilians are many: they may be eaten by large fish, owls, hawks, wading birds, snakes and water-hunting mammals such as raccoons and otters. However, once a young crocodilian reaches the age of about five and has grown to about 3ft (0.9m) in length, its chances of survival improve considerably. Nevertheless, even a mature crocodilian can be attacked and killed by other animals, mostly other predators, but even big, aggressive herbivorous species such as elephants and hippopotamuses may kill crocodiles in defence of their young. Some of the other enemies of crocodilians include tigers, leopards, large snakes and, of course, human beings. Crocodilians are not even immune from attack by their own kind;

cannibalism is common in various species, including American alligators (*Alligator mississippiensis*). This is especially the case when populations get too big and overcrowding occurs.

Crocodilians at Risk
It is extremely sad, but almost inevitable, that crocodilians are facing such an uncertain future, and it is almost entirely due to the impact of human beings. First, many are useful commodities: some are caught for their meat, which is often highly prized, and crocodile and alligator skins have long been used for making expensive leather items. Furthermore, because many crocodilians are large creatures, they are obvious and relatively easy targets for hunters. Second, they have earned a reputation as dangerous 'maneaters', which in the eyes of some almost justifies their persecution, whether the species is a threat or not. Third, the illegal trade in pet reptiles is seeing many rare species caught and smuggled out of their countries of origin,

The skin of a black caiman (Melanosuchus niger)*, the animal having been unlawfully poached in Amazonas, Brazil. This, the largest predator in the Amazon, is capable of growing to more than 20ft (6m) in length. It lives in a freshwater environment, which includes slow-moving rivers, streams, lakes and flooded wetlands.*

RIGHT
An American alligator
(Alligator mississippiensis)*, showing
the blunt head draped in
blanketweed.*

OPPOSITE
*The surfacing head of the estuarine
crocodile* (Crocodylus porosus) *on a
crocodile farm in Borneo.*

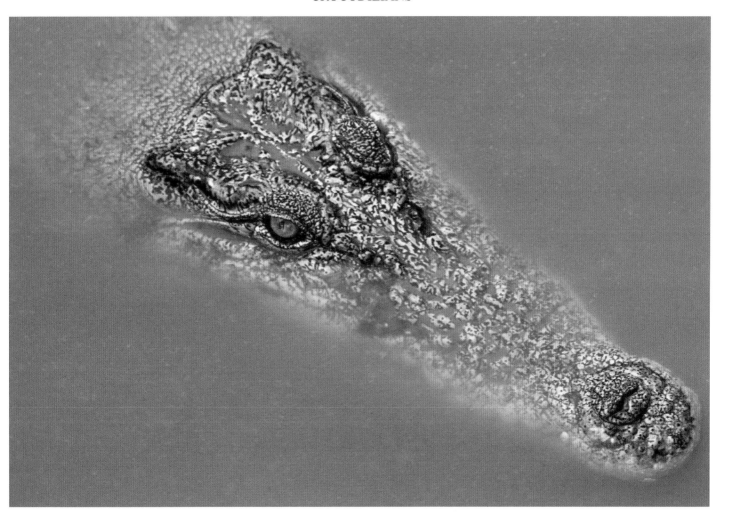

RIGHT
An American alligator appearing
through duckweed.

OPPOSITE
An American alligator basking
*among water lettuce (*Pistia
stratiotes*) in Corkscrew swamp,*
Florida.

when they often die, due to poor conditions in transit, while destruction of habitat is playing a big part in the reduction of many crocodilian populations. However, conservation programmes, legislation designed to protect vulnerable species and the creation of crocodile and alligator farms, where captive-bred species provide meat and leather instead of wild specimens, are among the measures designed to protect the remaining crocodilian populations.

CROCODILIAN FAMILIES

There are three families of living crocodilians and in all three there are members whose long-term prospects are at risk due to persecution or loss of habitat.

FAMILY ALLIGATORIDAE

This family contains the eight species of alligators and caimans. The word 'alligator' arose when the reptiles were first seen by Spanish explorers travelling in the New World in the 1500s, who referred to the beast as *el legarto*, 'the lizard'. Alligators and caimans have rather blunter snouts compared with the thinner, more triangular-shaped heads of crocodiles and the very elongated snout of the gharial. However, a more scientific way of distinguishing between alligators and crocodiles is by examining the jaws: it will be found that when an alligator's mouth is closed, the fourth tooth in the lower jaw cannot be seen because it fits into a socket in the upper jaw, whereas in crocodiles the tooth is still visible when the mouth is closed. As a family, the Alligatoridae range across the south-eastern U.S.A., Central and South

places that the crocodile can inhabit, and even around its river habitat it comes into conflict with rice farmers, especially when its habit of digging underground burrows undermine the roots of crops. There may be as few as 200 of these reptiles surviving in the wild and they are listed as critically endangered, although conservation programmes are in place to help maintain numbers.

Less at risk today is the American alligator (*Alligator mississippiensis*), which inhabits parts of Florida, Louisiana, Georgia and Texas in the south-eastern U.S.A., where it is found in marshes, rivers, swamps and other waterways, including the Florida Everglades; in 1987 it was named as the official state reptile of Florida. It was once seen to be losing a fighting battle against hunters and the destruction of its habitat, but the American alligator is now protected by law and its numbers are on the increase. It is not uncommon for people camping in areas populated by the reptile to discover a full-grown specimen wandering through their campsite. At other times, an American alligator may disturb a game of golf by wandering across the course, while some are even permanent residents on the lakes and ponds dotted around the campus of the University of Florida. Between 1973 and 1990, there were 127 reported attacks on human beings by American alligators, including a few fatalities, and there are numerous accounts of pets having been taken by them. Such events seem almost inevitable due to the fact that the alligator inhabits many places that human beings use for recreational activities, such as swimming,

America and China. Prehistoric, alligator-like reptiles probably first appeared on earth about 200 million ago, but the first members of the genus *Alligator* arose about 26 million years ago in North America. The caimans appeared about 65 million years ago.

The common or spectacled caiman (*Caiman crocodilus*) is the most widely distributed member of the family Alligatoridae. It has been introduced into a few places, such as the U.S.A., and it is found in a broad southern band from Mexico,

through most of Central America and into northern and central South America, including Brazil, where it lives in lakes and swamps. It can grow to a length of about 9ft (2.7m). The spectacled caiman gets its name because of the ridge on its head between the eyes that resembles the bridge of a pair of spectacles.

The Chinese alligator (*Alligator sinensis*) is one of the rarest and most vulnerable members of the family Alligatoridae. Today, the species survives only in areas surrounding China's lower Yangtse river. There are few wild

OPPOSITE
Detail of the teeth of Alligator mississipiensis.

LEFT
An American alligator devouring a racoon.

waterskiing and fishing. However, wildlife services offer plenty of good advice on how to avoid becoming a victim.

For example:

- Heed warning signs and don't swim outside designated bathing areas
- Always swim with another person
- Don't swim at night
- Avoid areas such as thick vegetation near riverbanks
- Don't feed or entice alligators

- Don't let pet dogs swim in areas that alligators are thought to frequent
- Don't remove, molest or attempt to kill alligators
- Inform official bodies such as the U.S. Game and Fresh Water Fish Commission of any incidence of alligators wandering in back yards or public places

FAMILY CROCODYLIDAE

There are 14 species of living crocodiles. The family arose during the late Cretaceous period about 65 million years ago, and quickly

spread throughout Europe, North and South America, Africa and Asia. Today, the family as a whole is also found in the East Indies and Australia. Included within the Crocodylidae are the biggest species (the estuarine crocodile *Crocodylus porosus*) and the smallest (Osborn's dwarf crocodile *Osteolaemus osborni*).

The family also includes the most widespread species, the Nile crocodile (*Crocodylus niloticus*), that ranges over most of Africa apart from the Sahara region. Up to 16.5-ft (5-m) long, the Nile crocodile inhabits

OPPOSITE
*An American crocodile (*Crocodylus acutus*), showing the long snout characteristic of this species.*

BELOW
*A saltwater (saltie) or estuarine crocodile (*Crocodylus porosus*) at Yellow Waters, Kakadu National Park, Australia.*

OPPOSITE and LEFT
*Nile crocodile (*Crocodylus
niloticus*).*

RIGHT
*An American crocodile (*Crocodylus
acutus*), with porcupine quills
embedded in its skin.*

*OPPOSITE LEFT, ABOVE and
BELOW*
*Yacaré (*Caiman yacare*).*

OPPOSITE RIGHT
*Nile crocodile (*Crocodylus
niloticus*).*

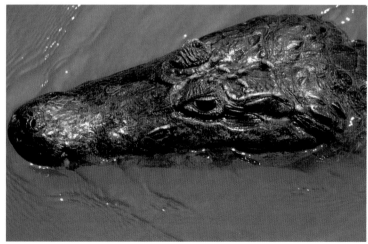

RIGHT
A female saltwater or estuarine crocodile carrying her baby.

OPPOSITE
An American crocodile in the Florida Everglades.

CROCODILIANS

BELOW
A Nile crocodile resting in shallow
water at the edge of Chobe river,
Botswana.

OPPOSITE
A rare albino Nile crocodile.

rivers, lakes and marshes throughout most of Africa excluding the Sahara. Large mammals and birds form the bulk of the Nile crocodile's prey, most of which are seized in the crocodile's huge jaws as they come to drink. After grabbing its victim, the Nile crocodile drowns it under water, then spins round while still holding onto the prey, twisting off chunks of flesh in the process. After a courtship display and mating, the female lays up to 75 eggs near the water, and guards them until they hatch.

The estuarine crocodile is found from India to Australia and is the most aquatic of the crocodiles. It has frequently been implicated in attacks on human beings. Ruthlessly hunted for its hide to make leather goods, the crocodile's large size makes it an even more tempting target.

The dwarf crocodile (*Osteolaemus tetraspis*) grows to a length of 5ft (1.5m), inhabiting streams and lakes in the west of Africa. It is sometimes called the short-nosed crocodile due to its extremely short snout, in

which respect it resembles an alligator.

This family also includes the false gharial (*Tomistoma schlegelii*) of South-East Asia, which gets its name because it bears a similarity to the true gharial (*Gavialis gangeticus*) of the family Gavialidae, having a long, thin snout armed with narrow teeth,.

Most members of this family have also been decimated through hunting and habitat loss, and conservation programmes are in force in an attempt to prevent numbers from dropping still further.

OPPOSITE and LEFT
*Nile crocodile (*Crocodylus
niloticus*).*

OPPOSITE
A mugger or marsh crocodile
*(*Crocodylus palustris*).*

LEFT
*Nile crocodile (*Crocodylus
niloticus*).*

Conservation status: the Philippine crocodile (*Crocodylus mindorensis*), the Orinoco crocodile (*Crocodylus intermedius*) and the Siamese crocodile (*Crocodylus siamensis*) are all classed as Critically Endangered; the Cuban crocodile (*Crocodylus rhombifer*) and the false gharial (*Tomistoma schlegelii*) are Endangered; the American crocodile (*Crocodylus acutus*), dwarf crocodile (*Osteolaemus tetraspis*) and mugger (*Crocodylus palustris*) are Vulnerable.

FAMILY GAVIALIDAE
There is only one species in this family, the gharial (*Gavialis gangeticus*), found in India, Nepal, Bangladesh and Pakistan. Males can grow to a length of 21.5ft (6.6m), although they are often slightly smaller than this; females grow to a maximum of about 13ft (4m). The gharial gets its name from the pot-like structure, or boss, on the end of the mature male's nose (in Hindi the word for 'pot' is *ghara*). The male gharial uses the boss to emit buzzing sounds that warn off rivals and attract mates at breeding time and feeds mainly on fish.

Conservation status: the gharial is classed as Endangered.

RIGHT
A warning of danger in South Africa.

OPPOSITE
A saltwater or estuarine crocodile (Crocodylus porosus) in the Kakadu National Park, Australia. This is the largest, in terms of weight, of all living reptiles.

CHAPTER EIGHT
REPTILES & MAN

A Chinese dragon batik.

Look at an engraving of an old mariner's chart from hundreds of years ago, and the chances are that it will be decorated with images of strange, imaginary serpents – potent warnings to sailors of the dangerous and mysterious monsters that inhabit the deep. This is an example of mankind's primeval fear of all things reptilian, a fear which has persisted for thousands of years and which exists to this day. It isn't even necessary for the threat to be real; it is simply enough to use a depiction of a snake-like creature as a general warning of great danger. However, it hasn't all been bad press for reptiles down the ages. In many cultures and civilizations reptiles were (and sometimes still are) revered, seen as tokens of good luck and even worshipped.

So what are the real dangers? The large snapping turtles have been known to give unwary bathers, or even people who keep them as pets, a nasty nip from their powerful, horny jaws, but most other turtles and tortoises are harmless enough. Most lizards scuttle away at the approach of a human being, and only two species – the Gila

monster (*Heloderma suspectum*) and the beaded lizard (*Heloderma horridum*) are venomous, although the poison is unlikely to kill a man. Moreover, both species live in remote places and only bite if provoked. The large common iguana (*Iguana iguana*) is a popular pet species, but does have a reputation for becoming spiteful as it grows older, sometimes lashing out with its powerful tail. The most feared reptile, as far as human beings are concerned, however, is the large Komodo dragon (*Varanus komodoensis*) of Indonesia. A bite from this can be extremely serious, and it is not unknown for a Komodo dragon to devour a human being. But again, the remoteness of its distribution makes it of limited danger to the human population.

Crocodiles and alligators certainly do attack and kill native fishermen, bathers and the unwary in places as diverse as Africa, India, Asia and the Americas. The Nile crocodile (*Crocodylus niloticus*) probably kills or injures several hundred people each year across its huge range, but the actual numbers are unknown. The American alligator (*Alligator mississippiensis*) has been responsible for nine fatalities in Florida since 1972, and the dangerous estuarine or saltwater crocodile (*Crocodylus porosus*) ate 12 people in Australia between 1980 and 1990.

Dangerous, even deadly, though some of the reptiles above may be, the statistics for attacks pale into insignificance when set against the numbers of fatalities caused each year by snakes. Although constricting cobras and pythons cause deaths each year, it is the venomous snakes that are mainly to blame. It is estimated that up to 100,000 people each

Alligator Bender, *Brookgreen gardens, South Carolina.*

year are killed throughout the world by snake bites, and many others are permanently handicapped by their injuries; but since many of these attacks take place in isolated rural areas and may not be reported accurately, the figure may be even higher. The most frequent attacks take place in South-East Asia, West Africa and parts of tropical America. Saw-scaled vipers (*Echis* species), Russell's viper (*Vipera russelli*) and the fer-de-lance (*Bothrops atrox*) are some of the species most often identified as responsible for attacks, although positive and accurate identification is often hard to prove, especially since the snake usually makes a rapid departure after it

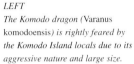

OPPOSITE
*Although a popular pet, the common iguana (*Iguana iguana*) can become aggressive and territorial with age.*

LEFT
*The Komodo dragon (*Varanus komodoensis*) is rightly feared by the Komodo Island locals due to its aggressive nature and large size.*

The Nile crocodile is responsible for many human deaths throughout Africa each year.

Don't risk your life

Large crocodiles inhabit these waters
- do not enter the water
- keep children away from water's edge
- clean fish away from water's edge and remove all waste

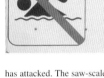

Australian National Parks and Wildlife Service

has attacked. The saw-scaled viper is found from the northern part of Africa through the Middle East to India, and is to blame for many of the human deaths from snake bites that occur in North Africa; it may even be responsible for more human deaths than any other species.

In many tropical countries, snakes often live in or around human dwellings. This is because they like to shelter in the vicinity of village houses, where there is ample food for them in the form of mice and rats. Although snakes are wary of human beings, it is easy to imagine how they can be inadvertently trodden on or disturbed in such situations, and it is hardly surprising when the snake retaliates in self-defence. The problem is often compounded by the fact that villagers wear little or no footwear that might otherwise protect them, and there is frequently no antidote to the snake venom available locally. People out hunter-gathering or working on farms and plantations are

equally at risk, often from the taipan (*Oxyuranus scutellatus*), which often lives near farms and sugar-cane plantations, where attacks on workers are common. Over 80 per cent of all snake bites in New Guinea are thought to come from these creatures.

The time it takes for death to occur after a person has been bitten, and assuming that no treatment is given, depends on the species. Cobra bites usually kill within eight hours; those of North American rattlesnakes take about 16 hours; kraits take 18 hours; the venom of Russell's viper can take about three days to have its full effect, and that of the saw-scaled viper works within five days. Often the best way to combat the effects of a snake bite is to administer an anti-venom serum, a drug designed to counteract the snake venom. The serum is made from the extracted venom of captured poisonous snakes, when the snake is first 'milked' – in other words, it is encouraged to bite a piece of leather stretched over a glass jar while being

carefully handled by experts. Venom flows into the jar and is collected, which is then freeze-dried and sold to laboratories that use it to produce the anti-venom serum, which is usually in the form of sheep or horse plasma that has been immunized with the venom.

Reptiles in Myth and Legend

No other creature figures more widely in the mythologies of the world than the snake. Of all reptiles, it is the snake that has provoked the greatest feelings of both revulsion and awe. It is also the animal that best evokes images of mystical power. Even to people living in places where the snake is not found, such as the Inuit of the frozen Arctic, the snake is still the subject of myths and legends, and although St. Patrick is said to have driven the snakes out of Ireland, he couldn't quite stop people talking about them. But why are snakes so fascinating? Is it the mysterious way they move, even though they are limbless? Is it their ability to bring sudden death? Is it the way they wrap themselves around their prey in a deathly embrace? Perhaps it is the cold, glassy, unblinking stare with which it fixes its victim, merciless and impassive as it goes about its deadly business? Or could it be its ability to engulf a creature far bigger than itself? It is probably a combination of all these things that distinguishes the snake as a strange and special creature.

The snake has been regarded with ambivalence in many cultures and ancient civilizations, including that of the Ancient Egyptians, in whose religious life animals played an important part. They believed

*Canebrake rattlesnake (*Crotalus horridus atricaudatus*). Rattlesnakes are responsible for most human deaths through snake bite in the U.S.A.*

certain animals to be the earthly incarnations of the gods and goddesses, and they were worshipped or feared accordingly. Venomous cobras and vipers probably killed many weak, young and aged Egyptians, death from a cobra bite being one of the oldest fates known to mankind. Pythons, too, often attacked small children, coiling around them and suffocating them in their cradles. Justifiably terrified of snakes, therefore, they expected every healer to have a repertoire of spells guaranteed to rid the body of snake poison; it is hardly surprising that the Egyptians used magic amulets to protect themselves, seeing that they regarded snakes as inhabitants of the underworld and inherently evil. The Pharaoh would often wear a representation of the wide-hooded cobra on his crown, possibly as

The venom of the grass snake (Natrix natrix) has no effect of human beings.

RIGHT
This painting is from a household shrine in Pompeii. It shows Bacchus, decked with grapes, standing before Mount Vesuvius. The snake is presented here as the genius loci *or spirit of the place.*

FAR RIGHT
A statue of Asclepius, Greek hero and god of healing, with the sacred serpent found at the sanctuary at Epidauros that was earlier sacred to his father, Apollo.

a form of protection or antidote and as a way of appeasing the god. In the *Book of the Dead,* however, the cobra is seen as the symbol of the earth, while the *ouroboros* is symbolic of wholeness or infinity in that it depicts a snake swallowing its own tail.

Biblical references to snakes are numerous and reflect the the way that reptiles were regarded. From the temptation of Eve by a serpent in the Garden of Eden and descriptions of corrupt judges 'like the poison of the serpent' to sinners in the New Testament being a 'generation of vipers', it is clear that snakes were the personification of all that was evil in mankind. Nevertheless, certain ancient Middle Eastern cultures also worshipped the snake, often using it as a rising from the chalice of St. John, while other iconographic images show it curled around the base of the Cross, symbolizing the triumph of good over evil. In Indian mythology, the demon known as Kaliya turned himself into a cobra and killed many people, but Krishna killed him and is often shown dancing on the head of a cobra.

Even without the religious associations snakes continue to figure highly in our modern society. From Kipling's *Jungle Book* to the ever-popular 'snakes and ladders' board game, the image of the snake endures. A well-known Italian car manufacturer

symbol of fertility, for example. Today, snake worship is still practised widely in parts of the world, including Asia and Africa. The snake has also featured in Christianity, depicted as

even features a snake on its badge.

Similarly, folklore and legends featuring lizards abound. As the witches in *Macbeth* stirred the ingredients into their magic potion, they made sure to add a lizard's leg to the concoction. In early Christianity, the chameleon was often used to symbolize Satan because he, like the chameleon, could change his appearance at will to deceive mankind, while in Dahomey, in West Africa, the chameleon is said to fetch fire from the sun. In some cultures, it is thought that chameleons do not eat, being nourished instead by the air. Furthermore, the curious,

FAR LEFT
The infant Horus, son of Isis and Osiris, shown as victor over crocodiles, snakes and scorpians.

LEFT
This wall painting is from a household shrine in Pompeii. The head of the household is in the centre with his head covered as part of a religious ritual and he is accompanied by two lares *(household gods). The* genius, *or guardian spirit of the house is represented by the snake.*

FAR LEFT
Laocoön, a Trojan priest, and his two sons struggle with the serpents that came from the sea and strangled them after Laocoön had voiced his suspicions regarding the wooden horse of Troy.

OPPOSITE
The chameleon's ability to change its appearance linked it to the Devil in early Christianity.

LEFT
Detail of Nine Dragon Wall, Beijing, China. 'Dragons' are a popular manifestation of our own fear and awe of reptiles.

Dragon boat on West Lake, Hangzhou, China.

independently swivelling eyes of the chameleon were considered by writers such as Pliny in the 1st century AD as proof that it was a talisman, able to restore sight to the blind. In ancient times, the Egyptians and the Greeks saw lizards as symbols of good fortune and divine wisdom. In Roman

mythology, lizards that hibernated over winter and then re-emerged in spring were supposed to symbolize both death and resurrection.

In the Christian tradition, the lizard was a symbol of the devil and of evil. The dragon in the St. George legend, and indeed many other dragons in the mythology of various cultures,

were probably all modelled on a typical lizard, though the addition of wings gave it a little extra kudos! Long, elaborate and impressive paper dragons are still used to celebrate the Chinese New Year or Spring Festival, when firecrackers are exploded to frighten evil spirits away. In Aboriginal

culture, it is said that the sky will fall if a lizard is killed, but among the Salish people of North America lizard tails were included as an ingredient of love potions.

One of the reasons why some lizards are persecuted or considered evil is because they are thought to be poisonous. However, this is only true of the two species of beaded lizards.

Among other reptiles, the turtle is also celebrated in myths, legends, fables and countless other stories. In classical mythology the turtle was renowned for its longevity but chided for its slowness, while in ancient China, the turtle was believed to have oracular powers. The turtle was synonymous with drought in Ancient Egypt, and a pair of turtles were sometimes depicted with a set of scales, representing the ebb and flow of the Nile's floodwaters. The ancient Greeks and Romans both considered the turtle to be a symbol of fertility, associating it with their goddesses of love, Aphrodite and Venus, who supposedly arose from the sea.

Our brief look at reptiles in mythology and their symbolism could hardly omit the crocodile, considered by many to be a treacherous and cold-hearted beast. The Egyptians saw it as the crocodile-headed god Sebek, who symbolized deceit, hypocrisy and treachery, among other questionable attributes. But the crocodile was also seen as a symbol of the sunrise and the fertile rising waters of the Nile. Pliny writes that the Romans revered the crocodile and were in awe of its stealth, while the Greeks saw the dual nature of human beings symbolized in it, demonstrated by the reptile's ability to live on both land and water.

FAR RIGHT
Tablets with turtles at their base in the Shanghai Provincial Museum.

*Cook Strait tuatara (*Sphenodon punctatus*), on Takapourewa, (Stephens Island), New Zealand.*

*Young Nile crocodiles (*Crocodylus niloticus*) at a crocodile farm in Zimbabwe.*

Reptiles as Pets

Not so very long ago, the most usual kinds of reptiles to be kept as pets were tortoises, terrapins, slow-worms and a few common species of lizards and snakes. Today, however, there are many more species available to the potential pet-owner. The availability of more specialized equipment and foods has made it possible to keep, and even breed, many species that were once considered too exotic and demanding for the average enthusiast. Unfortunately, many of these more unusual species have been taken from the wild, decimating numbers even more quickly than was once believed possible, through destruction of habitat and other environmental factors. This has inevitably led to stricter controls being placed on the trade in, and keeping of, certain reptiles. However, the illegal trade in species that are protected, or whose export is prohibited, still continues to

*The Mediterranean spur-thighed or Greek tortoise (*Testudo graeca ibera*), once the most popular of all reptiles kept as pets.*

be a major problem, and it is only the vigilance of customs authorities, conservation agencies and similar bodies that prevents the traffic in rare species from becoming even more widespread. Today, most of the exotic pets that have been legally supplied come from special captive-bred species, which prevents them from becoming rare in the wild.

National and international laws control the movement and keeping of many species. In the U.S.A., for example, the movement of some species between states is illegal, and there are laws that ban the sale of individual species under a certain size. To this end, the Convention on the International Trade in Endangered Species (CITES) governs the international trade in species and operates a licensing system, while the European Union also has controls in force to prevent the import of some species. There are also laws that prohibit the release of non-native species into the wild, which is very often a particular problem with reptiles, because sadly many people decide that once they have brought the animal home it is simply not suitable and decide to 'let it go'. Some snakes and lizards in particular tend to become aggressive as they mature, even those that are well-treated, and simply become too difficult for their owners to handle. Unfortunately, many such creatures released into the wild either die from lack of food, exposure to the elements or from attack by local, indigenous carnivores; conversely, they themselves may attack the wildlife inhabitants of the country, upsetting the balance of nature in the process.

It is not the intention, nor is it within the scope of this book to give advice on keeping individual species of reptiles; there are many excellent books on the market that cover the subject admirably. However, it is possible to include a brief survey of the range of reptiles available to the keen enthusiast. Overall, it should be remembered that caring for reptiles is a more demanding task than keeping other cage pets such as guinea pigs, gerbils or hamsters, or even cats and dogs. Many reptiles have very specialized requirements, and most failures experienced by pet-owners occur because the reptiles' living conditions have not been correct. Many reptiles are

*The slow-worm (*Anguis fragilis*) – another harmless reptile (in fact a lizard) frequently kept as a pet.*

BELOW: Image Jonas Bergsten public domain.

creating a self-substaining captive population that no longer relies upon wild caught animals, the individual keeper can make a significant contribution.'

In North America, the first to have hatched the threatened Egyptian tortoise is the Baltimore Zoo, whose Department of Herpetology has many other breeding programmes for endangered species and has set some longevity records for captives.

The Arizona-Sonoran Desert Museum, listed as one of the ten best in the country, has one of the most extensive living collections of native reptiles in the country, of which some are endangered, some are threatened, and some need special management. The museum also manages a Tortoise Adoption Program to serve the needs of desert tortoises in captivity.

North American box turtles have long been exploited in the pet trade and their numbers have drastically decreased, so much so that they are now protected in many areas of their range. U.S. Fish and Wildlife estimates that nearly 25,000 to 30,000 box turtles are exported each year, and since on average only two offspring of any given turtle will survive to adulthood in the wild, the rate of export is unsustainable and may endanger the survival of the species. 'The ultimate objective of most serious and conservation-minded reptile keepers is to achieve consistant and substainable captive reproduction; only in this way can we really justify the keeping of rare or endangered species in captivity.'(A.C. Highfield. *Keeping and Breeding Tortoises and Freshwater Turtles.*)

Many researchers believe that in the wild predators are responsible for destroying at least 80 per cent of all chelonian eggs laid and the babies that do hatch face additional dangers. Captive breeding reduces those dangers almost down to zero.

The batagur, a large herbivorous species found in South-East Asia is endangered due to extensive collecting of eggs and the killing of adults for food, while the African pancake tortoise is suspected of being endangered, vulnerable or rare. But there is no sufficient evidence to permit its classification.The Central American river turtle is vulnerable to endangerment because of its being hunted for its meat. Although to some degree protected by conservation laws, there is still much concern for its future.

Almost every species of seaturtle is either edangered or vulnerable and we can thank many shrimpers and commercial fisherman for this. Also in many civilizations, seaturtle meat is quite a delicacy and the eggs are ignorantly thought to be an aphrodisiac. The sale and consumption of turtles' eggs is a serious conservation problem in many countries and Islamic states. According to the Muslim religion, turtle meat is *haram* (forbidden) because the animal lives in land and water. However, this does not apply to turtle eggs, which are *halal* (permitted) because they are buried in sand.

Pollution is an added problem, so are carelessly discarded plastic bags from supermarkets.The diet of many seaturtles consists of jellyfish, and because they have

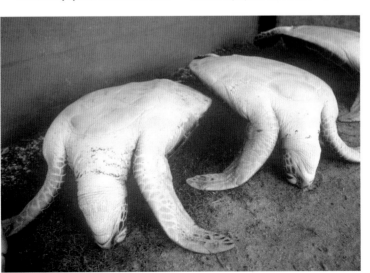

Scuba divers with the green turtle (Chelonia mydas) in Sipadan, Malaysia. Viewing rare creatures in their own habitat is far better than placing them in zoos.

poor eyesight they often mistake the bags for jellyfish and will suffocate as a result of trying to eat them. Moreover, the turtles' nesting areas are also being destroyed. It is very difficult for hatchlings to make it to adulthood what with all the predators stealing the eggs and snatching up hatchlings as they run to the water. In some parts, it is even illegal to touch a seaturtle. I used to live on South Padre Island in Texas, and at times would have sick turtles washed up on shore. It was well known there not to touch them, and to immediately call the Coastal Studies Laboratory located at the southern tip of the island. Among several of the endangered or vulnerable seaturtles are the leatherback, the green turtle, the loggerhead and the olive ridley, along with its close cousin the Kemp's ridley and the hawksbill.

Uncontrolled hunting of adults and excessive egg collecting has earned the Arru river turtle a spot on the endangered species list. It is now protected in most areas. The 12 tortoises of the Galapagos Islands are severely endangered. Sadly, one species, the Narborough Island tortoise, is already extinct.

The African spurred tortoise was rarely found as a pet up until about 20 years ago, but faced with adverse conditions during exportation and made to live in unsuitable climates, may of these will never make it and die. However, breeders today have successfully raised generations of the large, docile tortoises. With their survival in the wild in question, we at least know these turtles can thrive in captivity. They too are vulnerable to extinction.

Please be sure to stop for any turtle

SNAKES

The so-called harmless snakes are usually placid, although some of them may bite from time to time. Handling the boas, and in particular the pythons, needs extra care, partly on account of the size that some of them attain. They may also occasionally bite, but it is their powers of constriction that should be taken into special account when handling, when it is advisable for two adults to be present. Some of the best-known pet species are pythons (various species), boas (various species) and harmless snakes (various species such as rat snakes, gartersnakes, kingsnakes and bullsnakes).

Reptile Conservation

Many species of reptile have become endangered and some have even become

FAR LEFT
Children watching a green turtle returning to the sea at dawn on Heron Island, Great Barrier Reef, Australia.

BELOW
Site-markers for the eggs of green turtles collected on Talang Talang Besar Island, Sarawak.

species attempting to cross a road. Rather than place it back on the side of the road it came from, try your best to get it to the side for which it was heading. If you don't, chances are that it will try again when you leave it. Don't ever remove a turtle from its home range. Moving it to an area you may think as fitting may well be condemning it to an early death.

LIZARDS

Many species of lizards are kept as pets, though some, like the green iguana (*Iguana iguana*), can become large and aggressive as they mature. Among the best-known pet species are agamids (various species); anguids (such as the slow-worm *Anguis fragilis*), chameleons (various species), plated and flat lizards (various species), geckos (various species), iguanids (various species), lacertids (various species) and tegus.

RIGHT

RIGHT
'Brusher Mills', a New Forest snake-
catcher's grave in Brockenhurst
churchyard, England.

OPPOSITE
A felled rainforest in Brazil. Such
activities destroy the habitat of many
reptiles.

recently extinct, largely as a result of human
exploitation of one sort or another. Some
reptiles are caught for their flesh or their eggs,
and others are killed because their skins are
valuable or because their body parts are used
in fertility rites and other festivals. While
taking certain species of wild reptiles for the
pet trade results in the decimation of their
numbers, habitat destruction or interference
with the habitat for recreational, drainage and
other schemes is overall a larger threat to
many populations. Habitat destruction can be
particularly indiscriminate; for example,
felling tropical rainforests results in
destruction of the local ecosystem and the
loss of habitat for all the creatures in the
affected area.

Many of the world's most threatened
creatures, including reptiles, live in relatively
underdeveloped locations that also have large
populations of poor people. One of the
biggest problems facing national and
international conservation bodies is how to
reconcile the very real needs of the poorest
people who wish to exploit their natural
resources to earn an income – which often
means hunting the wildlife or destroying the
natural forests to create farmland – and
preserving their natural heritage, much of
which is unique. Even the introduction of
domestic animals such as dogs and livestock
can cause considerable damage to reptile
populations, since most lay their eggs on the
ground where they are especially vulnerable.
At sea, marine turtles are frequently killed
when they swim into the huge drift nets used
by modern fishing fleets.

As part of an overall strategy to help

RIGHT
*Slash and burn clearing of a
rainforest in Guyana, South
America.*

OPPOSITE
*An Egyptian cobra (*Naja haje*)
performing for a snake charmer in
Marrakech, Morocco. Such activity
is threatening the survival of this
species in the wild.*

protect and preserve all the world's plants and animals, governments must be encouraged to preserve their own natural wildlife heritage through better understanding of the needs of nature, the development of ecologically friendly industries such as 'responsible' tourism, and through grants and other incentives, if necessary, to generate forms of farming and industry for their people that do not necessitate reducing the habitats or the populations of the indigenous wildlife. In some parts of the world, such measures are already in place. For example, special farms or ranches keep and breed alligators and reptiles to supply the meat, skin and zoo trade. There are also places where visitors can see these creatures close up, without the need to encroach on their natural habitats in the wild. There are, of course, many success stories in the wild, too; in 1971, the natural population of the estuarine crocodile (*Crocodylus porosus*) in Australia's Northern Territory had been reduced by almost 95 per cent, but by 2001, following intensive conservation and education programmes, the population had returned to its former level of about 75,000 individuals.

INDEX

INDEX

INDEX

INDEX

INDEX

INDEX